Indoor Home Repairs Made Easy

Indoor Home Repairs Made Easy

PETER JONES

Butterick Publishing

Library of Congress Cataloging in Publication Data
Jones, Peter, 1934–
    Indoor home repairs made easy.
    Includes index.
    1. Dwellings—Maintenance and repair—
Amateurs' manuals.   I. Title.
TH4817.3.J66   643'.7   78-11348
ISBN 0-88421-088-X

Copyright © 1979 by
Butterick Publishing
708 Third Avenue
New York, New York 10017
A Division of American Can Company
Illustrations: Mark Richards
Book Design: Bobye List
Manufactured and printed in the United States of America.
Published simultaneously in the USA and Canada.

Contents

Introduction

IT DOESN'T MATTER WHO YOU ARE OR WHERE YOU live; you can be a pauper huddled in your cold-water flat or the reigning monarch of a palace, but sooner or later the building you live in will have a mechanical breakdown that demands the services of a plumber, an electrician or a carpenter. These yeomen of repair will dutifully arrive at your doorstep and, for a considerable fee, will solve almost any crisis. But believe it or not, the vast majority of those "crises" can easily be overcome by any sensible adult possessing no prior experience and a few ordinary tools.

Plumbers admit that easily 80% of the repairs they are summoned to make could have been performed by the homeowner. There are no mysteries to fixing a leaky faucet, for example — given a wrench, a screwdriver and a rubber washer, most drips can be eliminated in minutes, at a cost of pennies.

Electricians like to be a bit more elusive about all those wires they are always twisting together, but aside from the real danger of electrical shock, they have no basis for their attitude. True, electrical repairs are somewhat more complex than plumbing, but no more difficult, because electricians have been color coding the wires they use for years. So unless one is blind, most electrical repair work is well within the ability of the average adult.

Carpenters shrug if you ask them how much of their work could actually be done by a neophyte. Carpenters don't like to talk about what they do because the secret to their profession is so simple they can't understand why anyone hires them to repair anything.

Without taking away from the skills or knowledge of the mechanics who service your home, it should be noted that each of them pursues his various tasks with but one absolute, unbreakable, rigid rule that he unfailingly observes. As long as he obeys that one rule, he is bound to be successful.

For electricians, the rule is a law of nature: *electricity must always travel in a complete circle.* An electrician can splice all the wires he wishes in any manner he desires, and electricity will flow through them as long as it completes a circle. The power must return to its source.

The plumber may assemble any ingenious Rube Goldberg conglomeration of pipes he cares to dream up, and water will flow through them as long as he remembers that *every connection must be watertight.* He can even make water flow uphill, but he must never let any of it escape from between his pipes.

Carpenters have the hardest cross to bear. They must assemble more shapes, sizes and kinds of material than anyone else, so there are more opportunities to make mistakes. But the iron rule the carpenter must obey is that *every measurement must be precise.* Thus, if he is to cut a piece of wood 36½″ long, he must first be certain that this is exactly the length he needs. Then he must mark that length accurately on the wood. Finally, he must saw the wood precisely along the line he has inscribed.

If you fully understand the three rigid rules of repair and comprehend all their ramifications, there is nothing more that this or any other book can tell you. If you can apply the idea that electricity always travels in a complete circle or it will not travel at all; that the joint between two pipes must be watertight; that every measurement you make when assembling wood must be precisely executed; you can fix practically anything, in any home.

Admittedly, it helps if you have the right tools. But with only

15 of the countless tools available to you, you can perform some 90% of all the home repairs that ever arise.

The remainder of this book is devoted to providing you with demonstrations of the three basic principles, along with a few hints. It does not unfold any of those profound secrets that electricians, carpenters and plumbers tell only each other, for there actually are no secrets to unfold. There are only some variations on how you can go about meeting the rigid demands of the three basic principles.

The Author

ONE

Anatomy of a House

THERE ARE A GREAT MANY ELECTRICAL WIRES, plumbing pipes, thick pieces of wood, batts (or strips) of insulation and, occasionally, heating or ventilating ducts lurking within the walls and ceilings of every house. So when you are contemplating a repair to any part of the building, it is helpful to have at least a general idea of how the house is put together.

The construction of any house begins with a hole dug in the ground. The *foundation walls,* which will support the entire building, are made of stone, brick, concrete or, most likely, concrete blocks. They begin at the bottom of the hole and extend a foot or two above the ground. At that point the first wooden members are bolted along the top of the masonry to make up the *sill.* Normally, the sill is comprised of a pair of 2"x6" boards nailed together to complete a frame 4" wide and 6" high around the perimeter of the foundation.

The next member put into a house is the *girder,* which is the spine of the entire building. The girder extends over the center of the cellar and may be either several timbers nailed together or, better still, a steel I-beam. Either kind is supported roughly every 7' by *lally,* or *pipe, columns.*

Now come the *joists,* which are nailed across the top of the girder and reach from sill to sill. Joists are normally 2"x8" boards that have *bridging* nailed diagonally between them to help support the house and to prevent them from tilting under the weight they must hold.

A *subflooring*, or *deck*, is nailed to the top of the joists. The *flooring*, which is almost always a tongue-and-groove (T & G) hardwood such as oak or maple, is nailed on top of the subflooring.

Once the first-floor subflooring has been laid, the walls can be erected. Each wall consists of a 2"x4" *soleplate*, or *shoe*, which is nailed to the subflooring. Then 2"x4" *studs* are nailed vertically to the shoe and a pair of 2x4's are nailed together to form the *top plate*, which is attached across the top of the studs. Doors and windows are always framed by the wall studs as well as shorter *jack studs* and *headers*, which are the horizontal members that run between the studs.

As soon as the electrical and plumbing lines are installed between the studs and joists of the house, the framing is covered by *wallboard panels* on the inside of each room, and *sheathing* on the outside. If there is to be a second floor, it is built on top of the first-floor studs with its joists spanning the top plates of the first-floor walls. The joists are then covered with subflooring and flooring boards, and the walls are framed.

The *rafters* of a house can be attached in a number of ways. Most often they rest against the top plates of the top-floor walls and angle upward to meet at a *ridge pole*, which extends along the top of the roof and forms its peak. Once the rafters are in place, the entire structure is covered with sheathing-grade plywood or tongue-and-groove boards. Fifteen-pound *felt* (tarpaper) designed to moisture-proof the house, is then nailed to the sheathing, and the exterior siding and roofing materials are nailed on top of the paper.

Such is the general structure of every house. Within this structure there can arise many demands for repair or maintenance. Floor planks can become worn or broken, or loose enough to squeak. Electrical outlets can wear out and require replacing. Faucets can drip and sink drains become clogged. Walls can crack or be damaged by water. The building itself may settle on its foundation and cause doors or windows to stick or not close properly because their frames are pulled out of line. These and dozens of other small but annoying occurrences require repair and should be attended to as soon as possible. You could spend hundreds of dollars every year hiring all kinds of specialists to make these repairs. Or, for approximately $100 to $135, you can assemble a complement of 15 basic tools that will last you a lifetime and allow you to do most home repairs yourself with only the added cost of materials.

The anatomy of a house.

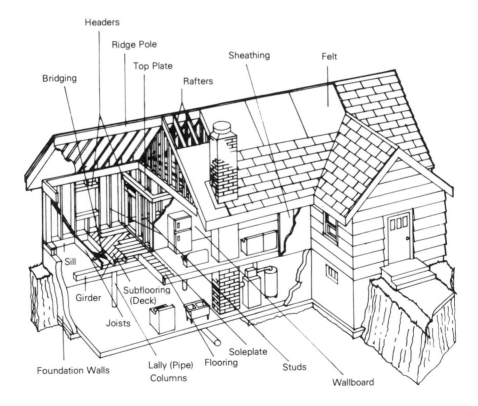

TWO

The 15 Basic Tools

THE TOOLS YOU NEED TO MAKE MOST HOME RE-
pairs do not have to be purchased all at the same time, although
it is a good idea to start out with at least a hammer, screwdriver,
rule, pliers and wrench. These five will probably serve you for
most minor problems, and the remaining 10 basic tools can be
added as the need for them arises.

SIXTEEN-OUNCE CLAW HAMMER

The purpose of a hammer is to bang nails into wood with one
end of its head, and to pull them out with the other. The reason
for spending $10 for a 16-ounce hammer is not so you can build
up your muscles, but so that you will have a weighty enough tool
in your hand to meet every emergency.

When you are nailing, grip the hammer near the end of its
handle and hold the nail in position between the thumb and fore-
finger of your other hand. Now tap the nail lightly until it is able

Claw hammer.

to stand up on its own. Then let go of the nail, and hammer it straight down. Your arm raises the tool and guides it toward the nailhead, but you can let the weight of the hammer do most of the work without exerting any great effort on the downward stroke. There is a rhythm to hammering nails and by the time you have driven three of them home, you will automatically establish that rhythm for yourself.

The claw side of the hammer head has a V-shaped slot in it so that it can grip any size nail. To remove a nail, hold the hammer upside down and catch the nail in the "V" of the claw, with the claw pointing away from you. Then rock the hammer toward you, using the curved top of its head as a fulcrum to pull the nail. You can also place a block of wood under the hammer head to give yourself more leverage when pulling long nails.

SCREWDRIVER

Screwdrivers can be purchased singly or in sets. A four-piece set, costing about $7, will give you one small, one medium and one large standard-blade screwdriver, along with a Phillips-head screwdriver; together, they ought to take care of just about every situation involving screws. There are no secrets to using a screwdriver. Screws are threaded so that they must be twisted clockwise when being set, and counterclockwise when being removed. The Phillips screwdriver has an X-shaped head rather than a single blade, and you will find that it is the only tool that will tighten or remove most of the screws used in home appliances and many machines.

Phillips Head

Standard Blade

Screwdrivers.

FOLDING RULE OR STEEL TAPE

You can buy a steel tape for $8 or a folding rule for $5. They are equally accurate, and you can use whichever you find more convenient. The folding rule is the carpenter's standby primarily because it can be handled easily without an assistant holding one end of it.

Folding rule and steel tape.

COMBINATION SQUARE

The combination square is perhaps the most versatile of all measuring tools, and costs about $7. It has a metal blade which is marked off in both inches and millimeters. The foot-long blade slides through a metal base and can be locked in any position. The base not only has 90° and 45° surfaces, but also contains a removable scriber for marking and a level for testing the level or plumb of any surface. The combination square can be used to check either the inside or outside squareness of surfaces, to mark and test a 45° angle and to draw accurate lines all over the place.

Sliding Rule

Tightening Screw

Bubble

Scribe

Combination square.

CLAMPS

C-Clamps

These clamps cost as little as 59¢ for the smallest size and go all the way up to $10. You will need at least two clamps that open to about 3″ and cost in the neighborhood of $5 each. Once you have used them, you will find that clamps are invaluable for holding together things that you are nailing or screwing, or while glue is drying.

There are several kinds of C-clamps, all of which have a variety of specialized purposes. *Bar clamps,* for example, are excellent for holding together a large project such as a chair. *Corner clamps* are almost mandatory when you need to hold two pieces of wood at right angles. *Spring clamps* are good for holding delicate projects.

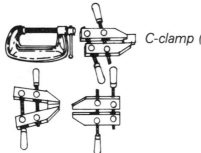 C-clamp (top left) and wood screw clamps.

Wood Screw Clamps

Even more versatile than C-clamps are wood screw clamps. These cost about $10 each and are well worth the money — they can be adjusted to almost any angle, giving you more complete control, because they are tightened with two screws rather than one.

Professionals make a habit of placing a piece of cloth, wood or even cardboard between their clamps and whatever they are clamping to avoid marring the wood of the workpiece. An even more reliable method is to glue pieces of felt to the jaws of all your clamps as soon as you buy them.

CHISEL

Chisels are available in any number of blade widths. If you buy only one, get a ¾″ width; however, one chisel will cost you $3.50, while a set of three is only $6. The set would include widths of ½″, ¾″ and 1″, giving you complete chiseling capability. Chisels are made specifically for gouging out bits of wood, and can be sharpened the same way you sharpen any knife. What you are not supposed to do with a chisel is use it as you would a screwdriver—this will nick the blade.

The chisel blade should be 9″ to 10½″ long, and the tool should have a plastic handle so that it can be hit with a hammer without being damaged. The flat, or unbeveled, side of the blade should be held against the wood when you are chiseling, but in tight places it is sometimes necessary to use the tool beveled edge down.

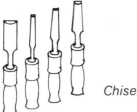

Chisels.

BLOCK PLANE

This tool, like the chisel, is used to reduce the size of wood. It is useful for a host of jobs, but is particularly handy when you are trying to make a door fit in its frame, to say nothing of framing and fitting shutters and windows. There are numerous plane sizes, but a 7½"-long block plane, which costs around $8, will do just about all the planing, beveling and camfering you will ever need.

The blade of a plane is removable, so it can be raised or lowered for different depths of cut as well as for replacing or sharpening. When you want to shave off a lot of material fast, first set the blade for a deep cut, then reset to remove less wood at a time as you near the end of the job. The blade is set by loosening the adjusting screw at the back of the tool and sliding the blade in or out of the slot in the base. The adjusting screw must be tightened as much as possible so that wood shavings are forced to curl away from the plane, rather than become jammed between the sides of the slot and the blade.

To plane with the grain, first clamp the wood to something stable so it will not move. Start the plane level and flat on the work and apply a steady, even pressure on the tool for your entire stroke. As long as you are planing with the grain, there will be a minimum of chipping and the work will not be too difficult.

Planing across the wood grain is harder to do and always leaves rough surfaces. When planing the end of a board, work from the edges toward the center, using short, chipping strokes; then plane off the hump left in the center of the wood. When you have reduced the end grain to size, you then have to sand the edge smooth.

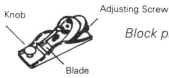

Knob

Adjusting Screw

Block plane.

Blade

SURFORM TOOL

You could buy a box full of files and rasps of varying coarsenesses, but for $5 you can also have a flat, file-type surform tool. The surforms will file and plane all kinds of wood, including end grains, as well as file aluminum, copper, brass, plastic and laminates. They are made in a variety of sizes and shapes, and they all have replaceable blades. The blades are actually strips of metal with sharp holes in them — like a cheese grater — and it is because of their multiple cutting edges that they are so versatile.

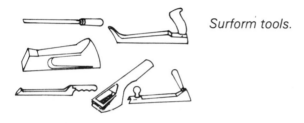

Surform tools.

PLIERS

Pliers come in many forms, but probably the most versatile are the *slip-joint pliers,* which cost $2 or so and are designed to grip nuts as wide as 2½".

What the slip-joint pliers are too big to handle the *needle-nosed pliers* can hold easily, particularly when you are working on switches, sockets, wires or any other electrical components. They cost about $6.50.

Slip-joint and needle-nosed pliers.

WRENCHES

While pliers are used to grip small objects like wires and nuts, wrenches are designed to get at such heavy-duty objects as drainpipes and bolts. There are two kinds of wrenches that belong in every home.

Adjustable Wrench

This has a thin head. For about $8 you can buy the 10″ size, which will handle anything up to 1⅛″ in diameter.

Pipe Wrench

This is an absolute necessity if you plan on doing any plumbing repairs. Buy at least an 18″ wrench. It will cost you around $8, and for that you can loosen every drainpipe nut in the house, or anything else that is 2½″ or less in diameter.

Pipe and adjustable wrenches.

TAPING KNIVES

These tools are used primarily for working with wallboard compound. They cost between $1 and $3, and their blades range in width from 2″ to 6″. At least buy a 2″ *putty knife,* which you can use when replacing window glass as well as for a variety of

Taping knives.

other prying and cleaning chores. You should also have a knife with a wider, 4″ blade for cleaning sticky substances, scraping wallpaper and applying wallboard compound, plaster or spackle.

ELECTRIC POWER DRILL

This is the first power tool most people buy, and for a very good reason: drilling through anything is long, hard work if you have to do it by hand. Besides, at a bottom price of about $8 you couldn't ask for a more complete tool; the drills come in ¼″, ½″ and ⅜″ chuck sizes and offer from ⅕ to ⅞ horsepower. The important element to bear in mind when buying a power drill is not what you will be drilling with it, but what other accessories you may want the machine to handle. A good ¼″ drill will do practically any kind of drilling and should cost around $15, but its power will not allow you to attach all the accessories available. Since you will most likely buy the accessories one by one as the need for them arises, it is wise to start out with a ⅜″ variable-speed machine, preferably with a reverse speed. The cost, however, will be upwards of $30 and if that is too much, do not feel badly about buying a less expensive, single-speed unit.

The drill is really a hand power plant that should last you for years. Besides drilling holes in everything from steel and wood to masonry, it will accept accessories that allow you to sand, drill around corners, pump water, remove rust, shape wood, trim laminates, saw, rout, buff, drive and loosen screws, and do almost anything else you can think of. Perhaps the first accessory to consider buying when you get the drill is a $2 *sanding disk*.

There is nothing awesome about using a power drill. Insert a bit in the drill chuck and lock it in place by tightening the chuck key. Hold the point of the bit against the object to be drilled, then

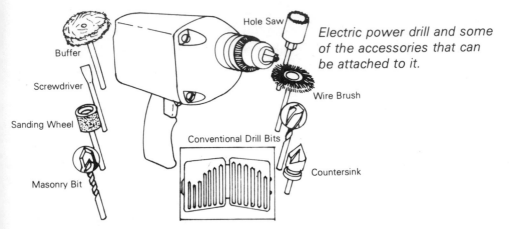

Buffer

Hole Saw

Screwdriver

Sanding Wheel

Wire Brush

Conventional Drill Bits

Masonry Bit

Countersink

Electric power drill and some of the accessories that can be attached to it.

pull the trigger and lean. You can use wood bits for wood, high-speed tempered-steel bits for metal. You will need a special masonry bit for drilling into brick or masonry; it costs between $1 and $3. But don't buy any of them until you need them.

SABER SAW

This is usually the second power tool that anyone buys. The secret to the saber saw is the blade you use, not the saw itself. You can buy a saber saw for as little as $9 or as much as $75. You can have one, two or several speeds, which is nice but not really necessary. Buying in the $15 to $30 range will get you a good-quality, rugged machine that lets you cut circles, rip, crosscut, bevel and, with the proper blade, saw up anything from cardboard to hardened steel. A set of 12 replacement blades costs about $6, and individual blades can be purchased for around $1 each. The blades, by the way, do break quite often, primarily because you will tend to inadvertently twist the saw when you are using it. Besides choosing the proper blade for the material you are cutting, there are two things to remember when using a saber saw: 1) When you are sawing, press straight down on the machine. A blade usually breaks because the user has allowed the back of the machine to lift into the air, where it can twist in his hand and snap the blade. 2) Anytime you are cutting a straight line, use the cutting guide that comes with the saw. If you are sawing too far away from the edge of the wood to use the guide, clamp a straight-edge along your cutting line and hold the saw against it as you work.

There are, of course, hundreds of other tools that can be added to your tool kit, and from time to time you will need a specialty tool to complete a particular project. You will also have to buy specific materials for specific tasks. But the 15 tools suggested here equip you to complete the vast majority of jobs to be done around any home.

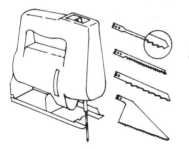

Saber saw and blades.

THREE

Working with Wood

PLANNING A PROJECT

Every home repair becomes a project. When you decide to make the repair, you can grab your tool kit and rush forth, waving your saber saw and swinging your hammer. But don't. You are liable to waste considerable time, effort and, perhaps, money. It is far wiser to sit down and contemplate the problem until you are sure of what must be done and how you intend to do it. As you think about the repair, answer these questions:

1) What, precisely, is the problem?

2) Do you have all of the right tools to do the work? If not, where can you beg, borrow or buy the tools you need?

3) Do you have all the materials — the right screws and drill bits, the proper adhesive, enough wood? If not, when and where can you get them, and for how much?

4) How will you proceed? Must something be dismantled? Is there an element to be built? Will you have to plaster, paint, fix pipes? Try to anticipate every step of the work.

5) How long will the repair take? Take a guess in terms of hours, and then double it. Repair projects have a habit of demanding more time than you would imagine. Whatever you think

is wrong is liable to be only part of the trouble, and once you begin work you may find some hidden surprises. A damp wall, for example, may not be just a matter of getting some sheetrock and replacing the stained spot. You may have to break open half the ceiling to locate and fix a leaking water pipe.

When you have listed every tool and material you think you will need, make sure they are all on hand before you start to work. Only then should you begin, in an orderly fashion, to tackle the job.

MEASURING, SQUARING, LEVELING AND PLUMBING

Measuring

The key to everything you do with wood is the accuracy of your measurements. Anytime you measure anything, do it at least three times. The secret to making accurate measurements is: assume nothing. Do not assume the walls are straight or that the window frame is square. Do not even assume that the pieces of lumber just delivered from your local lumberyard are truly square.

When measuring a large surface, measure it in at least three different places. The width of a wall, for example, should be measured at the ceiling, at the wall's center and along the floor. You will probably wind up with three different dimensions and have to strike an average.

Squaring

A question to ask when measuring is whether the object

under scrutiny is square or not. Use your combination square to determine both the inside and outside square of things. And don't be surprised if even your best furniture fails the test — furniture, like everything else in a house, can get out of line.

Leveling

You can do your measuring with a yardstick, school ruler, tape or carpenter's folding rule, all of which will tell you how wide, long, high or deep an object is. But another function of measuring is to find out whether something is absolutely vertical or exactly level. When an object is level, it is parallel with the ground, not with the floor, the ceiling or any other object. Place your combination square on, say, a shelf, and observe where the tiny bubble is in the tool's level. If the shelf is truly parallel to the ground the bubble will hover exactly between the two lines painted on the glass tube. If the bubble is closer to one end of the glass, that end of the shelf must be raised (or the opposite end of the shelf must be lowered). That is, the shelf must look tilted if you want it to be level.

You may prefer to leave your shelf crooked because if you straighten it, the crookedness of the rest of the room will make the shelf seem out of line. So while levelness is goodness, it is not always aesthetically desirable. This kind of situation arises often in older houses that have settled, dragging the frames around their doors and windows out of square. It is simple enough to remove the molding and correct the angle. But if you do that, how will the floor and ceiling, which are also tilted, look to the casual observer? You may find the way to reconcile perfection and reality is to straighten the molding only enough to make it *look* level.

Plumbing

There is another kind of leveling called plumbing. Something is plumb when it is absolutely vertical with the ground. The way you determine whether an object is plumb or not is to hang a string with a weight, such as a pair of scissors, on the bottom of it. When the string stops moving and the weight is motionless, the string will be vertical with the ground. If you hang a plumb from the ceiling in the corner of a room you will probably discover that the corner is crooked, or off plumb. But you can mark the plumb line on the wall; this will give you a vertical line to use as a starting point for accurately measuring anything on the wall.

MATERIALS

Lumber is divided into two basic categories: hardwood and softwood. *Hardwood* comes from any tree that loses its leaves in the fall, while *softwoods* are evergreens. In reality, many hardwoods, such as balsa, are actually softer than the softwoods, but generally hardwoods such as oak, cherry, maple, hickory and mahogany are tougher, closer grained and will take a stain or clear finish better than softwoods. However, softwoods such as pine, spruce, fir and cedar grow in abundance throughout America and can be reforested in relatively short periods of time, so you will encounter mostly softwoods in your local lumberyard.

Lumber is sold by either the board foot or lineal foot. The *lineal foot* refers to the real length of the board, measured in feet, and does not take into account its width or thickness. A *board foot* is 144 cubic inches, no matter what the shape of the wood, and is computed by multiplying width times thickness times length and dividing by 12. For a board 6″ wide, 1″ thick and 10′ long follow this formula:

$$\frac{6 \times 1 \times 10}{12} = \frac{60}{12} = 5 \text{ board feet.}$$

A board foot (top) is 144 cubic inches, no matter what the shape of the wood may be. Length is the only criterion for a lineal foot (bottom).

When you buy lumber, buy the smallest amount you can to complete your project, and pick the smallest standard size you can get away with. There is no advantage to buying a 12″-wide board that you mean to cut into two 6″-wide boards. To begin with, wider boards are scarcer, and therefore more expensive. Secondly, by the time you cut the board and smooth the edges of your cut, you will have two boards that are considerably less than 6″ wide.

Wood is sold in *nominal* sizes, even though the actual size is different. The nominal, or original, dimensions indicate what the board measured when it was cut at the sawmill. After it was cut its edges were planed and smoothed, and by the time it gets to your lumberyard it is about ¼″ thinner and ⅜″ narrower. Thus, the *actual* dimensions of a 2″x4″ piece are 1⅝″x3⅝″; a 1″x2″ piece is actually ¾″x1½″. When you are measuring a project, always consider the real (not the nominal) dimensions of the wood.

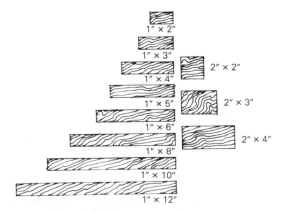

Common nominal *and* actual *wood sizes.*

When you get that wood home there are a few important things to remember about it. Wood, especially softwood, is stronger across the grain. The *grain* is created as the tree grows. Each year the tree adds a layer of tough, fibrous wood to its outer skin (just beneath the bark). The new skin produces *annular* (new growth) *rings* which are evidenced in any plank by dark wavy lines running in one direction along the wood. You can drive a chisel into the wood between its grain lines and split it; more importantly, you will discover that nails driven into the ends of a board — that is, in the same direction as the grain lines — have comparatively little holding power.

Another attribute of wood is that it swells and shrinks with every change in the humidity. A door that opens and closes perfectly all winter long will start sticking as soon as the first hot, humid summer day arrives. When you are fitting wood, measure it very carefully, taking into account that it will expand and contract all year round.

Plywood

Without question, the most versatile wood you can buy is plywood. Plywood is man-made, with three to seven thin layers of wood glued together under intense heat and pressure. Each layer, or *veneer,* is laid with its grain at right angles to the grains of the layers above and below it. As a result, a plywood panel is stronger, less apt to shrink, split or break, and in many ways is easier to work than any solid wood.

Plywood is sold in 4'x8' and 4'x10' panels made in thicknesses of $\frac{1}{8}''$, $\frac{1}{4}''$, $\frac{3}{8}''$, $\frac{1}{2}''$, $\frac{5}{8}''$, $\frac{3}{4}''$ and $\frac{13}{16}''$. They can be purchased as either exterior or interior types. *Exterior plywood* is assembled with a waterproof glue that allows the panel to be used outdoors. *Interior plywood* has a glue that is only water resistant, not waterproof, and should be used only inside.

Plywood is sanded on one or both of its face sides and requires very little preparation for painting or finishing. The face veneers are most often fir or pine, but at an extra cost you can buy panels that have maple, oak, cherry or even mahogany face veneers.

The difficulty in working with plywood lies in cutting it. It can be sawed easily, but the large size of the panels always presents a problem for the first few cuts. When possible, pay the extra cutting fee at your local lumberyard to have the panel rough-cut to something near the sizes you need. The edges will be rough, but a little sanding can give them a smooth texture.

CUTTING AND JOINING

You can cut any wood with your saber saw. To maintain a straight line either use the saw guide, or clamp a piece of straight-edged wood along your cut line and saw with the edge of the saw's base plate held against the straightedge.

Cutting joints with a saber saw is almost impossible; any complicated joint must be made with your chisel. Except when using dowels, the joint you will most often need to make is the simple *butt*. To form a butt joint, the edges of two pieces of wood are brought together, usually at right angles, and held in place with a combination of nails or screws and glue. The most successful joints occur when the edges of the two butting pieces touch at all points. To achieve this, you will probably have to plane, file or sand the edges until they are absolutely flat.

All points of the two pieces should be touching for a good butt joint.

Nails

Nails come in all sizes and shapes; there is a type of nail for nearly every situation. As a rule, you need be concerned only with common and finishing nails. The *common nail* has a wide, flat head and is used whenever it does not matter whether the head is seen or not. The *finishing nail* has a smaller head which can be driven beneath the surface of the wood and then hidden by filling the hole with wood putty or plastic wood. Finishing nails are used whenever you want the nails to be as unobtrusive as possible. To *countersink,* or hide, finishing nails, place the point of a common nail or *nail set* (which costs about $1) in the indentation in the head of the finishing nail; tap two or three times with your hammer until the finishing nail is below the surface of the wood. Then cover the nail with wood filler.

CHOOSING NAILS. A nail holds two pieces of wood together with friction, so the more nail surface touching the wood, the better it will hold. You can get more nail surface against the wood by using a long thin nail, a short thick one or one with ridges or grooves in its shank. If, however, the nail is too thick, it may split the wood; if it is too long, it may stick out of the wood.

When choosing nails, select one that is no more than three

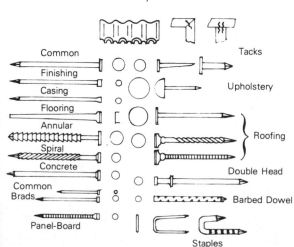

Nail sizes and shapes.

Common
Finishing
Casing
Flooring
Annular
Spiral
Concrete
Common
Brads
Panel-Board

Tacks
Upholstery
Roofing
Double Head
Barbed Dowel
Staples

How to countersink a finishing nail:
1) *Stop hammering when nailhead is slightly above surface;*
2) *drive head below surface with nail set or common nail, then fill in recess with filler.*

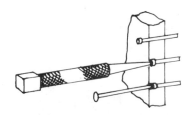

times as long as the thickness of the first piece of wood it will enter. For a piece of ¾″-thick wood you would use a nail no more than 2¼″ long.

DRIVING NAILS. Where and how you drive a nail is almost as important as the nail size. Anytime you nail *across* the grain of the wood, the nail will have more holding power and the wood is less likely to split. But if you drive a nail into the ends of the board, or *with* the grain, the nail will have almost no holding power and will be easy to pull out.

Two good rules to remember about nailing are: 1) Whenever possible, drive a nail into the wood at an angle, that is, *toenail* it. If you are putting more than one nail in the wood (every joint should have at least two nails), drive them at different angles so they can reinforce each other. 2) Always situate a nail so that the load it bears will fall across its shank, rather than along its length, or it will drive the nail in deeper.

Screws

The advantage that screws have over nails is that they hold the wood together with the many tiny surfaces in their threads, rather than by sheer friction. Screws usually make a neater, stronger joint because they tend to draw the wood tightly together. The bad news about screws is that you generally have to drill a preliminary pilot hole for each one.

Screws are made of steel, brass, galvanized metal, copper or bronze, and are designated by a code number that has no relation to anything. They are numbered from 0 to 24, with each number offered in a range of lengths. When buying some you would say,

Some ways of properly driving nails into wood.
Nails driven into wood at an angle are said to be toenailed.

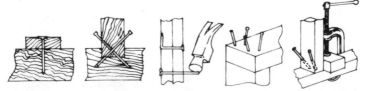

"Six #12's, 1¾" long." The length you need is determined by the thickness of the pieces of wood you are assembling—never use a screw that is longer than the combined thickness of the two pieces.

When you know what length you need, you must choose from the three types of screw heads available to you. *Round* and *oval heads* have flat undersides and are meant to remain above the surface of the wood; use them anyplace you don't care about seeing them. *Flathead screws* have a beveled underside so that they can be driven below the surface of the wood, then covered over and hidden.

SOME HINTS ABOUT SCREWS. When you are drilling a pilot hole for any screw the question arises, "How big should the hole be?" Screws get their holding power only from their threads, not from the shank that holds them. To determine the proper size drill bit for a screw, hold a bit against the threaded part of the screw. If you cannot see the screw threads above and below the bit, the bit is too big. Try smaller bits until you can see the threads.

When you want to *countersink* a screw, first drill the pilot hole. Then put a bit the same diameter as the screw head on your drill and bore ¼" into the pilot hole. You can also buy a specially designed bit called a countersink for your drill; this will prevent drilling too deeply into the wood.

Select your screwdriver carefully. It should have the longest barrel possible, to give you the greatest possible leverage. The

---

Screw shapes and types.

Flathead

Oval Head

Round Head

Phillips Head

Dome Head

Dowel

The proper size bit for any screw can be placed next to the threaded portion of the screw and will allow you to see the threads above and below it.

blade should fit snugly in the slot of the screw head and not overlap it. If the blade is too small in the slot it will slip and batter the slot, making it difficult to turn the screw. Damaged screw slots can sometimes be repaired by running a small file or hacksaw blade through them. If that fails, discard the screw.

You will also encounter the saga of the stuck screw that refuses to be removed. There are two approaches to this problem: 1) Try turning the screw clockwise, tightening it, then counterclockwise, loosening it. Keep tightening and loosening the head until the screw comes free. 2) Heat the screw head with the tip of a soldering gun or flatiron. Heat expands metal, and as the screw cools it should shrink away from whatever is holding it tight.

Heavy-Duty Fasteners

There will be times when nails or screws are not strong enough for the job and you need something bulkier, such as lag or carriage bolts. *Carriage bolts* have coarse threads and a round head which is either flat or conical; the conical ones can be countersunk. You do not drive carriage bolts into the wood. You first

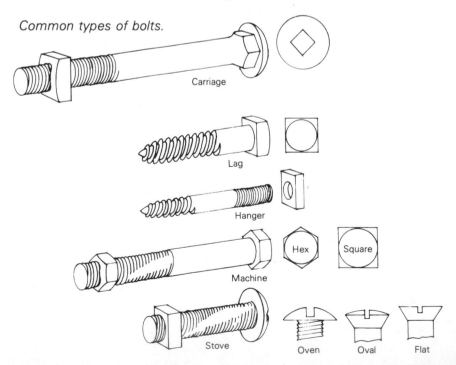

Common types of bolts.

Carriage

Lag

Hanger

Machine   Hex   Square

Stove   Oven   Oval   Flat

drill holes for them and then, using pliers or an adjustable wrench, tighten the nut that threads onto their shafts.

In situations requiring outsized screws, use *lag bolts*. These are threaded and driven into a pilot hole with a wrench. They come in lengths of up to 16″ and can be as much as 1″ in diameter.

Finally, there are *hanger bolts*. Half of their shaft is machined to accept a nut, and the pointed end has a screw-type thread. These are perfect if you know the location of wall studs and you want to hang, say, a cabinet. Drill a pilot hole for the screw half of the hanger bolts, screw them in with pliers or a wrench, then fasten the cabinet to the wall by inserting the bolts through holes in its back.

When it comes to hanging things on a brick or concrete wall, you can often use flat *masonry nails*, which are driven directly into the masonry. These nails are fine for securing 1″x2″ strips to hold a sheetrock wall, but if something heavier, such as bookshelves, is to go on the wall, go to one of the *expansion plugs*. These fasteners can be plastic or fiber sheaths, or lead plugs that are inserted in a predrilled hole in the wall to provide a gripping base for a screw. The screw forces the plug to expand and grip the sides of the hole. When you are drilling the plug hole, use a carbide-tipped masonry bit that is the same diameter as the plug. Regular bits will not work.

Hollow walls require a different kind of fastener known as a *toggle bolt, molly* or *collapsible anchor*. Again, you have

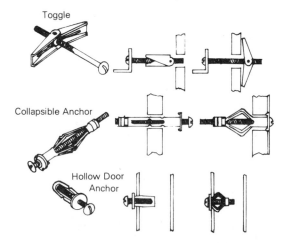

Toggle

Collapsible Anchor

Hollow Door Anchor

Some anchors used with hollow walls, and how they work.

to drill a hole large enough to accommodate the fastener when its gripper is folded back against its threaded bolt, as shown in the illustration. Once the unit is inside the wall it springs open and is forced against the back of the wallboard as you tighten the bolt.

Adhesives

There are dozens of adhesives on the market, and you can find one for any glue job. But it can be difficult to decide which adhesive you should use for what. Many glues come in powder form and must first be mixed with water. Others are in liquid form and can be used straight from their containers. Still others have two substances that must be mixed together. Glue manufacturers are very precise about their products, telling you exactly what the adhesive will glue and how to use it. Follow the directions on the package closely. Here is a general rundown on adhesives and what they will do, along with one or two product names for each category.

LIQUID RESINS (e.g., Elmer's, DuPont glues).   These are the white glues, made with a polyvinyl emulsion which is not waterproof but which makes them suitable for wood, cork and leather. They are good all-purpose glues, especially when used with nails or screws.

ALIPHATIC GLUES (e.g., Titebond, Se-Cur-It glues).   These are the cream-colored glues, and are better all-purpose glues than the whites — they set faster and are stronger. They should be clamped for at least an hour.

PLASTIC RESINS (e.g., Weldwood, Elmer's plastic resins).   These come as a powder to be mixed with water. They are resistant to water and work well on wood, particleboard and veneers. They must be clamped for at least 12 hours.

CASEIN GLUES (e.g., National Casein Co. No. 30 glue).   These are made from milk curd and are strong, water-resistant glues that are excellent for woods. They are mixed with water, and set best at low temperatures. Clamp for six hours. *Caution:* Caseins may stain some woods.

RESORCINOLS (e.g., Elmer's Waterproof, U.S. Plywood Waterproof resorcinol glues).   These are waterproof and strong. They come as a powder catalyst and a liquid resin which have to be mixed. They require clamping for 10 hours.

EPOXIES (e.g., Weldwood, Devcan Clear epoxies).   These have two liquid components, a resin and a catalyst, which must be mixed. They should be clamped for about 10 hours, but they will hold anything and are resistant to both heat and moisture.

SUPERGLUES (e.g., Krazy, Duro Super glues).   These will bond most plastics, metals, vinyl, brick, tile and rubber, but not paper, fabric or wood. Don't use them on polyethylene or Teflon finishes. They set in seconds and cure within half an hour.

HOT MELT GLUE.   This glue comes in round 2"- to 2½"-long sticks which are inserted into an electric glue gun (which costs $8 to $15). The glue melts at 380°F, squirts out the nozzle of the gun and dries to 90% of its strength in 60 seconds. You use up a lot of glue sticks quickly, but the hot melts will hold anything, including upholstery, ceramics, Formica surfaces and leather. With a one-minute setting time, you can just hold two pieces together rather than clamp them. The drawback is that only small areas can be glued at a time.

CONTACT CEMENTS (e.g., Weldwood, Goodyear contact cements).   These are used for bonding laminated plastics to counter tops. Both surfaces to be bonded are coated, and the cement is allowed 15 to 20 minutes to dry. Then the surfaces are brought together and instantly adhere.

CLAMPING GLUED PARTS.   Clamps are particularly useful for keeping together two pieces of wood while glue dries. The important thing about clamping is: don't tighten the clamp too much. It is not true that the tighter something is clamped, the better the glue will dry. If the two pieces of wood are squeezed too tightly most of the glue will be forced out of the joint, leaving insufficient adhesive to hold the wood together. Tighten your clamps only until the pieces are held firmly in place. If the glue has been properly spread over the joint, it will begin to squeeze out at that point, indicating that the clamp is just tight enough.

Wood Fillers

Wood putty, plastic wood and a host of similar products are used to fill cracks, splits and holes in wood. All these materials are applied in the same manner. Push them into the offending crevice with a putty knife or your fingers, leaving the material piled slightly above the surface of the wood. When the material dries, sand it level with the wood. Sometimes your first application of filler dries with an indentation at its center. If so, add a second layer of filler.

All fillers can be sanded, will accept paint and harden to a tough, brittle texture. There are advocates for every brand, so experiment with several kinds until you find the one you prefer.

COVERING PLYWOOD

There are several ways to hide plywood edges. Fillers can be applied along the edges of a plywood board to artfully hide the layers of veneer. You can glue on a strip of wood veneer (sold in ¾"- to 2"-wide strips), or tack on a narrow strip of solid wood. Plywood edges, like all end grains, do not offer good holding power for nails and they soak up glue as if they were sponges. Whatever you attach to an end grain should be both glued and nailed. The glue should be applied to the edge and allowed to dry. This first application, which has soaked into the wood, provides a base for the second coating to adhere to.

The best nails to use with plywood ends are the screw-type panel-board nails. These come in a wide range of colors, and are between ¾" and 1½" long. They are spiraled like screws, and will dig into the wood and tenaciously refuse to come out.

Molding

Still another way of covering plywood edges is with decorative molding, but molding has other uses as well. It is used around the frames of doors and windows, along baseboards, and to cover the joints between walls and ceilings. Traditionally, molding pieces are joined with either a mitered or beveled joint. To make either cut you will find it more accurate if you can place the molding in a miter box (which costs about $5) and cut it with a utility saw. If you plan to work with a lot of molding, both the miter box and the utility saw (which often comes with two or three different blades) are useful tools to have around.

To cut molding, simply lay it in the miter box at the appropriate angled slot and work your saw through the slots. You can use any long, thin finishing nail to hold your molding in place and, except on furniture or plywood ends, the molding need not be glued. When the molding is in place, use a common nail or nail set to countersink the finishing nails.

 A miter box is invaluable for making miter or bevel cuts.

FURNITURE REPAIR

In addition to the repairs that must be done to your house, troubles with your furniture must be dealt with. Most of these problems can be fixed simply, but require patience. Furniture is out front. Everybody sees it, so any repair work you do on it must be as inconspicuous as you can make it. That means you have to work carefully and neatly.

Regluing Laminated Counter Tops

The laminated counter tops in your bathroom and kitchen are made with either a plywood or composite-board base; the plastic laminate was glued to the base with contact cement. If an entire edge or top piece has come loose, reglue it by applying contact cement to both the base and the laminate. Allow the cement to dry for about 20 minutes. Then place a sheet of waxed or brown paper on the base and lay the laminate *exactly* where you want it to be glued. Slide the paper out a few inches at a time while pressing down on the laminate. The laminate will stick immediately and there is no way you can unglue it, so make certain you have put it where you want it.

If only part of the laminate is loose along an edge, you cannot get contact cement between the pieces and keep them apart long enough for the cement to dry. As an alternative, squirt either a white or a cream glue into the split and clamp or weight the piece in place long enough for the glue to dry.

Repairing Split or Broken Furniture Wood

Furniture wood that is split or has pieces broken off can be glued back in place by first cleaning off all the old glue, then using one of the epoxies, plastic resin glues or any other extra-strong glue. The repair must then be clamped. Since furniture is liable to have some weird and wonderful shapes in it, you may have to resort to holding pieces together with masking tape, or wrapping string around the repair and twisting a screwdriver or small piece of wood through the string to tighten.

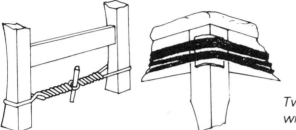

Two ways of clamping without using clamps.

Redoweling

Every winter the cold air outside and the warm air in your house combine to work apart the backs and legs of your furniture. Sometimes the parts are assembled with joints; most often, when a part falls off, you will discover dowels. The basic principles of regluing apply, but when you have a dowel in the middle of a joint you are in for a little more work. The holes where the dowel resides must be cleaned of all old glue before any new adhesive can adhere to the wood, and if the dowel is broken you may have some problems getting it out of its socket.

REMOVING DOWELS. If the dowel is intact or if enough of it protrudes from the wood to hold with pliers, grip the dowel and twist as you pull it out of its hole. If the dowel is broken off, try driving a small nail into its center, then grip the nail with your pliers and pull the dowel out of its socket. If that fails, use a drill bit that is slightly smaller than the diameter of the dowel and drill into it. You want to be careful to drill only the dowel, not the furniture wood, so keep your drill straight and don't go deeper than ½". Then scrape out whatever pieces of the dowel are left in the hole, using a nail, ice pick or anything you can get into the hole.

After the dowel is removed, thoroughly clean the socket of all the old glue. Do this by using a piece of sandpaper rolled around the eraser of a pencil or simply rolled into a tight cylinder. The dowel itself must also be scraped clean of old glue and then sanded.

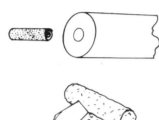

All old glue must be cleaned from a dowel and its socket before regluing.

GLUING DOWELS.   Presuming the dowel is intact and secure in one of the two furniture pieces that have come apart, coat the dowel with glue, then apply the adhesive to the hole. Smear glue on both sides of the wood around the dowel and reassemble the pieces, clamping them. Always apply more glue than you need; excess glue will ooze out of joints and can be wiped off immediately with a damp cloth. If glue does not come out of the joint as you clamp it, remove the clamp and add more glue.

USING NEW DOWELS.   Dowels are made of hardwood or plastic, and sometimes have a spiral groove cut in their barrel which allows the glue to travel along its length. They can be purchased at many large hardware stores and lumberyards for less than $2 for 100. They range from ⅛" to 1" in diameter and come in lengths of up to 2". If you cannot find any individual dowels you will have to buy a 2'- or 4'-long dowel stick at your lumberyard and cut it yourself. If you have a broken dowel in hand, take it with you when you go shopping to be certain your new dowels are the right diameter.

If you are merely replacing a broken dowel, your only problem is to cut the new dowel to proper length. After removing the broken dowel, measure the depth of both sockets. Cut the dowel ⅛" shorter than the combined depths of the sockets. Put the cut dowel in the sockets and assemble the furniture pieces to be certain the dowel is not too long, preventing the pieces from coming together. Then disassemble the pieces and glue the dowel in place.

Adding new dowels to furniture is rarely necessary, unless you are joining a broken piece of wood and a dowel can help strengthen the repair. It is a tricky (but not difficult) chore to drill two holes in two different pieces of wood so that they are at right angles to each other and perfectly in line. The secret weapon here is a set of seven doweling centers, which costs less than $2. The centers have a sharp point in the exact middle of their caps which is used for marking the center of the opposite hole.

 *Doweling centers.*

To add a new dowel, begin by drilling a hole the diameter of your dowel into one of the furniture pieces forming the joint. Try to position the hole with as much wood around it as possible, and avoid drilling too deeply — ½" or so will suffice. When the first hole is drilled, insert in it whichever dowel center fits snugly in the hole. Now bring the two pieces together, making sure you align them perfectly. The point in the middle of the dowel center will make a small indentation on the opposite piece of wood — that indentation marks the center of your second socket.

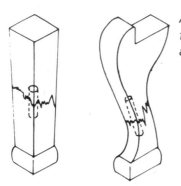

A dowel inserted in the center of a broken furniture part, such as a chair leg, will appreciably strengthen the repair.

When you drill the second hole, be careful to hold your drill at the same angle used on the first. When both sockets are drilled, preassemble the dowel and pieces to be sure they fit properly. If your drilling is off angle, you can enlarge one of the holes somewhat to make the proper fit.

Fixing Chair Rungs

Chair and table rungs are actually huge dowels. If they come out of their sockets but still fit snugly when you reinsert them, clean out the socket and the rung tip, and reglue. If the rung fits loosely in the socket, clean the rung end and give it a thin coat of glue, then wrap thread around the end, add more glue, and fit it into the socket. If the thread is not enough, saw a slot across the end of the rung and tap a wedge-shaped piece of wood into the slot to widen the rung end. Then glue the rung in place.

Loose-fitting rung ends can be split and spread apart with tiny wedges to make them fit snugly in their sockets.

FOUR

Doors and Windows

THE HOLES THAT ARE MADE IN WALL FRAMING FOR both doors and windows are known as *rough openings*. They are shaped to their proper size by nailing *trimmers*, or *supporting studs*, to the existing wall studs. The top of the rough opening is formed by a *header*, which is made by nailing two 2x4's together and cutting them to span the top of the door or window.

DOORS

Once the studs and header are in place, the door frame is filled in with ¾" stock that forms the *jambs*, and strips of molding that stop the door when it is closed. Decorative trim that surrounds the door is then added.

Types of Doors

FLUSH DOORS. These have a smooth surface on both sides, and can be either *solid wood* or *hollow*. If they are hollow, they have a solid wood frame which is stuffed with corrugated cardboard and then covered by a ⅛" plywood veneer. Hollow doors

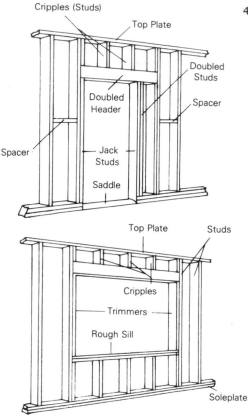

Doors and windows are always completely framed by studs and headers.

are nearly always 1¾″ thick and can be purchased at most lumberyards for between $10 and $15. Solid flush doors are made with a core of two or more plywood panels, and covered by a decorative veneer on both sides. They cost between $20 and $50.

SASH DOORS. The sash door is constructed with a wooden frame that holds one or more panels. They come in a whole range of styles and, as a rule, are sold in either 1⅜″ or 1¾″ thicknesses.

Measuring Doors

Measurements for a new door should be taken from the top of the *saddle* to the *head jamb* on the frame, and from side jamb

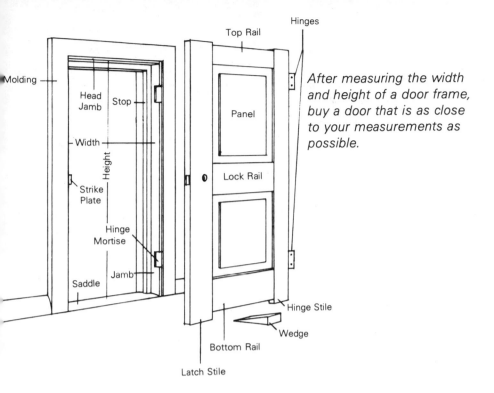

Molding

Head Jamb

Stop

Width

Height

Strike Plate

Hinge Mortise

Jamb

Saddle

Top Rail

Hinges

Panel

Lock Rail

After measuring the width and height of a door frame, buy a door that is as close to your measurements as possible.

Hinge Stile

Wedge

Bottom Rail

Latch Stile

to side jamb. Take all of your measurements at least three times to be sure they are correct, and then buy a door that is as close to your dimensions as possible. All doors come in widths of 12″ to 42″ and lengths of up to 8′, so the closer you get to the exact size you need, the less planing you will have to do.

Installing Doors

It doesn't matter whether you are hanging a solid oak front door or louvres on a closet; the chore of putting up a door is laborious, time-consuming and frustrating, even for professionals. The frustration comes not from the procedure, but from the fact that you are working with a large object that must be shaved down to within fractions of an inch, and there is a very small margin for mistakes if the door is to open and close properly when you are finished. So begin with the assumption that it will take you all afternoon to hang one door, and follow these steps:

1) Remove the existing door, strike plate and hinges.

2) Measure and plane the new door to size. Sash doors come with their side stiles extended beyond the top and bottom rails; these stile extensions must be trimmed off with a saw or plane. Allow ⅛" clearance at the top and on each side of the door, and ¼" at the bottom. If the door is to open over a rug, allow ⅞" for clearance at the bottom. As you are planing the latch side of the door, bevel it slightly toward the stop side, that is, the side of the door that first enters the frame when the door is closed. The *stops* are those thin strips of wood nailed to the center of the frame to keep the door from closing past the lock.

3) Stand the door in its frame. If it does not fit, plane the sides until it does. It is better to shave off only a little at a time between repeated fittings than to try and make the door fit after the first planing and risk having the door too small.

4) Once the door fits in the frame with a full ⅛" clearance on either side, slide a piece of wood under the bottom rail to elevate it at least ¼" above the saddle. Now mark the position of the hinges. The top hinge should be 6" to 7" from the top of the door and the bottom hinge 10" to 12" from the floor. If there is a middle hinge, position it equidistant from the others. Be sure to mark the hinge positions on both the door and the jamb before you remove the door from the frame.

5) If the existing mortises in the door jamb are in good condition they can be reused, but first fill all the screw holes with slivers of wood coated with cream glue.

6) The size of the mortises to be cut in the door are determined by holding one leaf of the hinge in place against the wood and tracing it. Doors are normally hung with butt hinges that are between 2½" and 4" long. When you place the butt on the wood, the barrel of the hinge should hang over the inner face of the door.

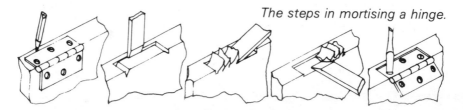

The steps in mortising a hinge.

Now score your outline of the hinge with a chisel held vertically and driven straight into the wood to a depth equal to the thickness of the leaf (about ⅛"). Using short, shallow cuts, chisel out the wood inside the scored lines and make the bottom of the mortise as flat and even as you can. Fit the hinge leaf into your mortise. The metal should be level with the wood around it. If the leaf is too high, make the mortise deeper; if the mortise is too deep, shim it up by putting cardboard under the hinge. Drill pilot holes for the hinge screws and screw the hinge into place.

7) Mortise the door jamb, if necessary, following the procedure outlined above in Step 6. Stand the door in place, attaching it to the jamb with a single screw in each of the hinges. Test-swing the door; if it opens and closes properly, put the rest of the screws in the hinges. (You should be so lucky the first time.)

If the door does not close properly you have a number of options. First, be sure the hinges are neither too high nor too low in their mortises. All the hinge leaves on both the door and the jamb must be absolutely flush with the wood around them.

Next, check to see if the hinges cannot close completely because the hinge side of the door is getting in the way. Plane the door edge at a slight angle toward the door stop side. Naturally, beveling the hinge edge will make your mortises shallower, so now you will have to deepen them.

Finally, see if the door stop is too close to the edges of the new door, preventing it from closing. If so, pry the stop off the jamb and reposition it so it is out of the way.

Repairing Doors

Most of the repair work you will have to do on doors is a matter of sanding or planing edges or shoring up hinges. Here is a quick reference list of common door ailments and what you can do to cure them.

Loose hinges	Remove the hinge screws and plug their holes with wood splinters dipped in cream glue. Reset the screws in the hinges.
Door binds	Carefully plane the binding edge.
Door binds at *top* of latch edge	Loosen the *lower* hinge screws. Slide cardboard under the hinge and retighten the screws.
Door binds at *bottom* of latch edge	Loosen the *upper* hinge screws. Slide cardboard under the hinge and retighten the screws.
Door binds at top	Plane the top of the door. (You may have to remove the door.)
Door binds at bottom	Remove the door and plane the bottom.
Door binds along latch or hinge side	Remove the hinges from the door and plane the hinge side. To plane the latch side, first remove the lock.
Door opens by itself	Loosen the strike-plate screws and place cardboard under the plate. Retighten the screws.

Locks

INSTALLING LOCKS. Essentially, installation of a doorknob-and-lock combination requires drilling one large hole through the faces of the door and a smaller hole through a mortise in its edge. Then a third hole is drilled in the jamb under the strike plate. The exact positioning of these holes depends on the type of lock you are installing and is explained in detailed instructions that accompany almost any lock sold today. To follow the manufacturer's instructions, however, you will have to buy a hole-saw attachment for your drill that can cut a 2½″-diameter hole.

TYPES OF LOCKS. There are three basic lock types used on doors found in the home: mortise, rim and cylindrical. All three have key cylinders with the exception of tubular locks, which are a version of the cylinder type and used for interior doors.

 Mortise locks have a spring-loaded latch as well as a dead bolt, which is pushed in place by the key to double-latch the door. Mortise locks can be installed only in doors that are at least 1⅜″ thick.

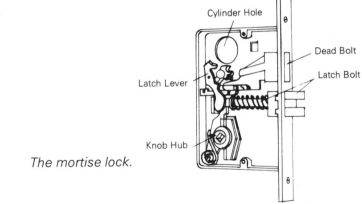

Cylinder Hole

Dead Bolt

Latch Bolt

Latch Lever

Knob Hub

The mortise lock.

 Rim locks are mounted on the inside face of the door and may have either a dead bolt or a spring-loaded latch that locks automatically. The lock case is positioned on the door behind a hole for the cylinder, which is drilled through the face of the door.

Cylindrical locks consist of a keyway inserted in the knob and a set of pin tumblers that allow the cylinder to rotate, either opening or locking the latch. The inside knob has either a push button or revolving lever that can lock the door.

Tubular locks are a lighter-duty version of the cylindrical lock and are normally used on interior doors. The latch can be locked by pushing a button on the inside knob, but can also be released from the outside by pushing a rod or nail into a small hole in the center of the knob.

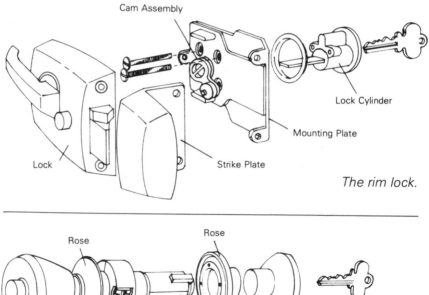

The rim lock.

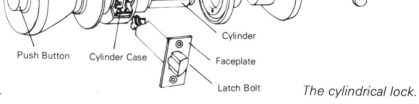

The cylindrical lock.

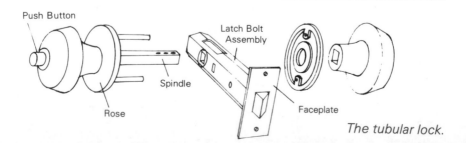

The tubular lock.

MAINTAINING LOCKS.   You can clean any lock with paint thinner or grease solvent. Then lubricate it with powdered graphite, silicone spray or a light oil. Lubricate the tumbler pins by blowing graphite into the keyhole, or apply graphite to the key and work it in the keyway. *Never* put oil in a cylinder — it will make the tumblers stick.

Here are some common problems with locks and how to deal with them.

Key will not enter cylinder	Hold the key over a flame. Insert warm key into the cylinder. Repeat heating and inserting key until it is fully seated in place. Turn the key carefully and slowly to free the tumblers.
Key partially turns; bolt does not move	Relocate strike plate if it is binding against the bolt. Check the bolt for paint or dirt jamming it. Clean all foreign matter off the bolt, then lubricate.
Part of broken key stuck in keyway	Loosen the setscrews and remove the cylinder from the lock. Hold the cylinder downward and tap the back of it. Or insert a thin, hooked wire in the top of the keyway and pull out the key part.
Cylinder out of line	Loosen the setscrews and rotate the cylinder slightly to the correct position.

Duplicate key being used	Try the lock with the original key and if that works, have the duplicate recut.
Wrong key used, or the lock has been picked	In either case, the tumblers may be damaged and have to be replaced.

WINDOWS

Without question, windows are the biggest energy wasters in any home. Nevertheless, when properly installed, located and used, windows can actually reduce the cost of heating and cooling a house. For example, a window positioned on the south side of a house might be used for solar collection to hold down the expense of winter heating. Then again, that same window will increase air conditioning costs unless it is also designed to block out heat in summer.

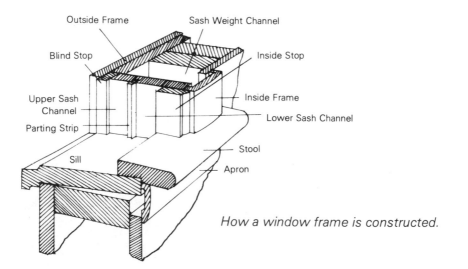

How a window frame is constructed.

There are several tricks for making a window modify its action each season. One method is to plant a shade tree in front of it. Other ways are to use draperies or venetian blinds, or to install an awning. Or you can cover it with a "summer storm window" that has tinted glass to cut down ultraviolet light transmission, yet allows daylight into the house.

The major decision you have to make about windows is whether to upgrade your leaky, inefficient, single-pane windows and shield them with storms, or replace the windows altogether with double- or triple-pane, higher-efficiency units. Consider the possibilities carefully from the point of view of reduced heating

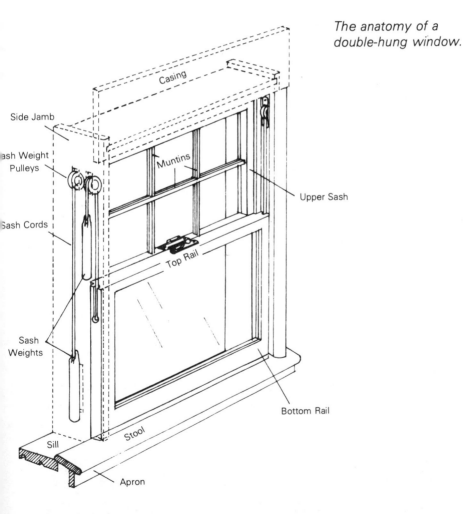

The anatomy of a double-hung window.

and cooling bills, as well as aesthetics. Replacing prime windows is also far more expensive than adding storms, but then again, the best storm window available will not totally insulate a worn-out prime window.

The most common window found in homes is the *double-hung window*. It is called double-hung because it has an upper (outside) sash and a lower (inside) sash, both of which slide up and down in the window frame with the help of sash weights hidden behind the side jambs. The basic design is centuries old, but as you can see in the illustration, the construction of the frame has become rather intricate during its evolution.

Double-hung windows are particularly vulnerable to the elements because they usually are made with wooden frames. They can settle, warp, sag and just plain rot out, causing gaps that are an invitation for both air and water to enter the house. Seeping water initiates an irreversible process of wood rot; the cold air rushing through the house will increase your fuel bills by as much as 20% a year.

Keeping Out Water

Examine the exterior joints where the window frame meets the outside building wall. There should be no gaps; if the old caulking is cracked or missing, follow this procedure:

1) Renail any loose wood in the window frame.

2) Scrape out any loose caulking and dirt lodged between the wood and the wall, using a wire brush and putty knife.

3) Insert a generous bead of caulking (about ⅜″ in diameter) into the joint. You can do this by hand, but learning to use a caulking gun (which costs $2) takes almost no practice, and the gun is quicker and neater.

If any part of the gap in a joint is too wide to support the caulking (more than ½″) you will first have to stuff the hole with oakum, which is a caulking string available at most hardware and all plumbing supply stores.

4) Allow the caulking to dry for at least two days or until a skin has formed on its surface, then paint.

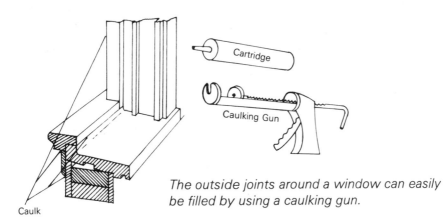

Cartridge

Caulking Gun

Caulk

The outside joints around a window can easily be filled by using a caulking gun.

Repairing Exterior Cracks and Holes

Examine the outside of the frames and sills for any open holes or cracks. These should be brushed with either linseed or tung oil, then filled with putty. If the paint is cracked and peeling, remove it with a wire brush and repaint the wood surface.

If the paint has peeled to the extent that a lot of bare wood is showing, you'll have to waterproof the entire frame before you repaint it. The waterproofing is done by applying any preservative containing pentachlorophenol. Pour it on generously until the wood cannot absorb any more of the liquid. The wood preservative acts as both a sealant and a water repellent, and also provides better adhesion for any paint that you put over it. Allow the preservative to dry for 24 hours before you do any painting.

Repairing Putty

The putty around a windowpane is supposed to keep water from seeping into the wooden frame, where it will promptly rot out the wood. However, you have to have an absolutely tight seal between putty and glass, or the putty won't do any good at all.

When you are replacing old putty, first chip away all loose or cracked putty and remove any dirt or debris from the putty channel. When the channel is absolutely clean, paint the exposed wood with boiled (as opposed to pure) linseed oil, which will retard the drying and cracking of new putty. Now lay a bead of glazier's putty along the channel and press it into the corner with your putty knife so that it forms about a 45° angle between the wood and the face of the glass.

Fixing Window Sills

There are several recognized procedures for giving a tired window sill added years of life, and all of them work toward creating a surface that will shed — not absorb — water. Your aim is to fill all cracks and create a smooth, continuous surface that slopes away from the house so that water will not flow back against the window frame.

The most accepted way of reconditioning a window sill, assuming it has cracks and holes but is intact, is to first scrape away all loose material. You can do this with a putty knife, wire brush or any tool that will clean the sill thoroughly. Once the sill is clean, soak it with pentachlorophenol wood preservative, then wait 24 hours and saturate the wood with boiled linseed oil. Fill in all cracks and holes with wood putty and wait at least two days before priming and painting.

Keeping Cold Air Out

Unfortunately, the best time to find air leaks is during the winter, when you can hold your hand near the window frame and instantly know exactly where air is coming through. But winter is an uncomfortable time of year to do anything about a leaky window. While the weather is still warm look for places where the sash does not appear to be sealed tightly. The sash should fit snugly in its side frames. The bottom of the upper sash should mate tightly with the top of the lower sash. The upper sash should close snugly against the top of the frame. The bottom of the lower sash ought to shut tightly against the sill.

Anyplace the windows do not fit exactly is a guaranteed source of air leak. If you don't need to open the window during cold months, the simplest method of coping with air gaps is to caulk them. Use rolled caulking and press it into all the crevices around the inside of the window, then forget it until spring. If the window must be operational during cold weather, tack weather-stripping to the inside of the window frame. Weatherstripping is effective but rather unsightly, so there are some alternative ways of using it:

1) Gaps at the top and bottom of the window can be sealed by attaching adhesive-backed foam to the top of the upper sash and the bottom of the lower sash. If the foam strips refuse to stick because of grime on the sashes, give the wood a coating of contact cement before pressing the foam in place.

2) Gaps between upper and lower sashes can be sealed by tacking a strip of felt or spring bronze to the inside edge of the lower sash.

3) Windows that have a lot of play at the sides can have weatherstripping tacked to the side channels without removing the sash from the frame (just raise and lower the sash). The weatherstripping can be felt strips, zinc fringed with felt, or spring bronze.

In addition to the spaces that occur in window frames, an astounding amount of cold air can leak in under the inside moldings around the window casing. Often these leaks leave a telltale dirt mark on the wall that will show where to fill the joint with wallboard joint compound.

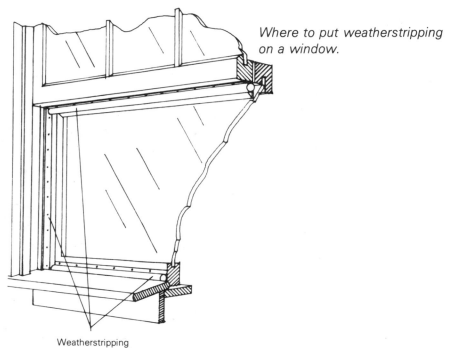

Where to put weatherstripping on a window.

Weatherstripping

Care and Nurture of Window Sashes

Any open joint lets in water, but window sashes are particularly vulnerable to water damage. The outside joints between wood and glass are normally protected by putty, but when the putty deteriorates, considerable moisture can leak into the wood itself. During cold weather, windows are subject to inside condensation which runs down the glass and into the wood, causing the paint to peel and the wood to rot.

FREEING SASHES. The most bothersome thing that happens to sashes is that they get stuck and will not open. Freeing window sashes can be a chore. If the sash moves, but grudgingly, rub hard soap or paraffin along the edges of the blind stop, the inside stop and the parting strip to act as a lubricant. If the sash does not move at all, it is most likely because the frame has swollen or been painted shut. You can break the paint seal by hammering the blade of a 4" taping knife or a chisel between the parting strip and the window sash. If this fails to free the sash, carefully pry off the strips of wood that hold the lower sash in place. If the upper sash must be removed, the parting strips between the two sashes must be pried loose. Sand or plane the strips to make them a fraction of an inch smaller and then replace them exactly where they were. This effectively widens the channel so that the sashes can move freely.

REPAIRING LOOSE JOINTS. When you have taken off the parting strips, you can remove the sashes for inspection simply by lifting them out of the frame.

Examine the corners of the sash where the rails come together for any loose joints. Often you can close these simply by pushing them together. Otherwise, tightly wrap cord around the frame to tighten the joints. Once the rails are together, screw flat metal reinforcement angles against the inside of the corner. Be certain to leave enough clearance between the metal and the edge of the frame so that the frame can slide back inside the parting strip. Alternatively, if the condition of the rails allows, the corners can be reinforced by drilling holes and tapping in dowels coated

When you reassemble a sash, use glue on the joints and on whatever fastener you have chosen.

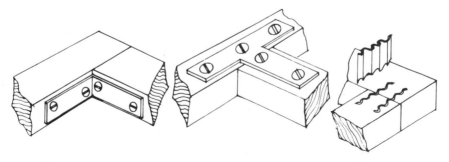

with a waterproof exterior-grade glue. For that matter, if the joints are open and clean they can simply be reglued and clamped, or corrugated fasteners can be hammered into the top of the joint.

All loose or cracked putty around the panes should be removed and the cleaned area given a coat of boiled linseed oil before any new putty is applied.

PROBLEMS WITH PAINT. If the sash has been unpainted for years, not only may the paint be cracked and peeling, but the bare wood has probably dried and fissured.

Remove the sash by prying off a stop on one side of the frame and swinging the sash outward. Scrape off all loose paint and thoroughly saturate the bare wood with a mixture of 50% boiled linseed oil and 50% turpentine. Allow the sash to stand for 24 hours and repeat the soaking process. Let the sash dry for two more days; then plug all the holes and cracks you can find with putty, and prime for painting. You can use any high-quality oil-base exterior paint.

When the paint on the *inside* of a sash peels there is not much you can do about it except install storm windows. The peeling is caused by moisture coming either from the outside or from condensation that forms during cold weather. You can preserve the sash by treating the wood so that it will absorb only a minimum of moisture.

Scrape away all peeling, loose or flaking paint, then saturate the wood with a mixture of 50% turpentine and 50% boiled linseed oil. Apply the mixture every two or three days until the wood will no longer absorb it, then fill all cracks and holes with linseed oil putty and allow it to dry for at least a week. Prime and paint with a high-quality oil-base paint.

INSTALLING NEW GLASS PANES. The hardest part of replacing a pane of glass is getting rid of the old putty. The rabbetted grooves that hold the glass must be cleaned down to the bare wood, but inevitably there will be chunks of putty so tough that even attacking them with a hammer and chisel does not work. If the chisel technique fails, you only have two recourses: 1) Heat softens putty. Apply the tip of an iron wrapped in tin foil (to keep the tip from becoming gummed) to the putty. 2) Some chemicals soften putty; these include paint remover, lacquer thinner and muriatic acid. Feel free to try them.

When the sash is finally cleaned, measure the length and width of the hole along the inside edge of the rabbetted grooves. Deduct ⅛" from both the length and the width of the hole to allow for irregularities in the wood and for its expansion and contraction during weather changes. Buy a glass pane that meets your measurements.

To set the glass you can use either linseed oil putty or latex putty, commonly known as glazing compound. Either will do a satisfactory job, but if you choose the glazing compound, the rabbetted groove in the sash must first be primed with any paint, which is allowed to dry. If linseed oil putty is the choice, simply brush the rabbets with boiled linseed oil. The oil will soak into the wood and give the putty a base it can adhere to.

When glass is placed in the sash, it should not touch the wood, but float in a bed of putty so that it is completely sealed against moisture and won't rattle. To make the putty bed, spread a ¹⁄₁₆" layer of putty on the bottom and sides of the rabbetted grooves, then press the glass gently into the grooves to distribute the putty evenly. Be sure there are no air gaps anywhere under the glass.

Next, set glazier's points into the wood around the glass, using either the traditional metal triangles, the newer push points or just plain brads. The metal fasteners, not the putty, actually hold the glass in place, so the points should be tapped partway in every 8" to 10" along each side.

When the glass is firmly in place, make rolls of putty and

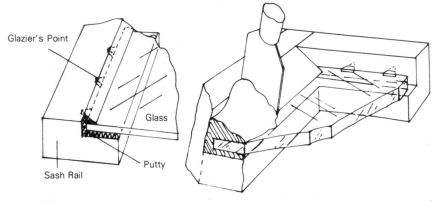

The cross section of a window frame. Note that the glass pane is placed on a bed of putty and held in place with glazier's points, which are covered by still more putty.

press them around the edges of the pane. Form a smooth bevel by pressing the putty down firmly with your putty knife. Then draw the knife slowly along the putty to even out the bevel.

It is essential that the knife blade be kept clean if you want to achieve a smooth bevel. The best way to do this is to wipe the blade from time to time on a pad of steel wool moistened with linseed oil. The bevel should not extend beyond the rabbetted edge of the sash or in any way be visible from inside the house.

Paint is vital to the durability of putty. It should be applied after the putty has dried for at least three or four days. The paint should extend ⅛" over the putty onto the glass so that it makes a watertight seal. You can guarantee a straight paint line by sticking masking tape to the glass a fraction of an inch away from the putty.

FIVE

Problems with Floors and Stairs

FLOORS

Most recently built floors consist of a ¾″-thick *underlayment*, or *deck*, made of plywood or tongue-and-groove planks nailed across the supporting joists. The flooring is then nailed to the deck and is almost always tongue-and-groove oak or other hardwood. The flooring is sold at most large lumberyards, and any board that must be replaced can usually be matched.

However, if you want to match the floorboards in an old house, forget it. Many old houses have 1″-thick pine floors which

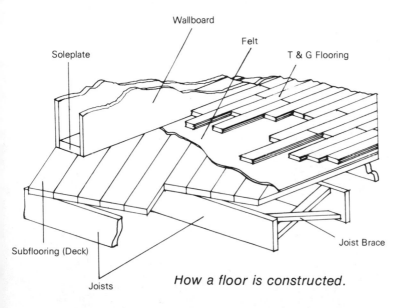

How a floor is constructed.

/ 65

may or may not be tongue and groove, and usually do not have a deck under them. You cannot purchase 1″-thick pine boards anymore, so if you have to repair the floors in a historic house you must resort to some artfully disguised trickery.

Getting Rid of Squeaks

Floors will develop squeaks anytime a board is loose, the nails stop holding or the house shifts. The quickest way to locate a squeak is to walk on the floor and stop the moment you hear a noise. If you find the board under your foot is loose, toenail 2″-long spiral or annular ring flooring nails into the end of the plank. Normally, the floorboards meet directly over a joist, so any nails driven within an inch of the ends of the floorboards should have more than just the subflooring to hold them. The nails should all be countersunk and covered with wood putty.

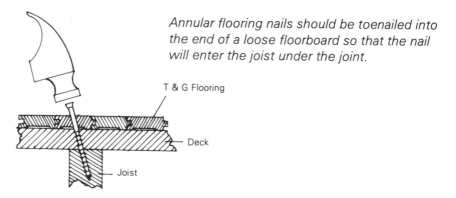

Annular flooring nails should be toenailed into the end of a loose floorboard so that the nail will enter the joist under the joint.

T & G Flooring

Deck

Joist

Replacing Damaged Floorboards

Replacing a broken section of floorboard presents a problem in that the board is most likely a tongue-and-groove construction and cannot simply be lifted out of its position. In order to remove the broken section, drill a series of overlapping holes across the board on both sides of the broken section without boring too deeply into the subflooring. Now split the board lengthwise between the holes with your chisel, and remove the pieces. Square the ragged ends of the remaining board (where the drill holes were made) with a rasp. Then measure and cut your replacement board so that it fits tightly into the hole. When the new board is cut, turn it over and chisel off the bottom half of its groove. Apply glue to the tongue of the new board as well as to the remaining part of the groove, and insert the new wood in place. Nail it to the subflooring, countersink the nails and cover them with wood putty. Finish the new board to match the rest of the floor.

The sneaky tricks department goes to work when you have to replace an old pine plank. If the hole you are filling spans two or more joists and the planking is not tongue and groove, your problem is that new pine planks are ¾″ thick, which is ¼″ thinner than the old boards. All you really have to do is place ¼″-thick pieces of wood on top of the joists before inserting the new board and nailing it in place. You might want to use ¾″ pine plywood instead of pine boards, particularly if you are replacing a 12″- or 14″-wide board.

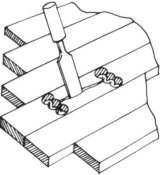

Drill holes across both ends of a damaged floorboard, then use your chisel to split the board and remove it.

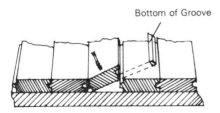

Bottom of Groove

The bottom half of the floorboard groove must be chiseled off before a replacement board can be put in position.

If you are filling in a small section of old pine board that spans any joists and there is no subflooring to rely on, get out your drill, saber saw and C-clamps. Cut two narrow strips of ¾" plywood or pine (scrap pieces of 1"x2" furring will do). The strips should be long enough to extend 4" crosswise beyond each side of the hole you are filling, and are clamped under the hole at each end. With the clamps holding the furring tightly against the underside of the floor, drill pilot holes through the flooring into the 1x2's and countersink at least two screws in each end of both strips before removing the clamps. Fill the screw holes with wood putty.

You have now given the hole a secure subflooring. Cut a piece of board that will fit snugly into the hole. If it is not as thick as the existing floorboards, shim it by placing ¼"-thick pieces of wood on the furring strips before you insert the replacement plank. When nailing the patch, drive your nails at a sharp angle and hammer easily so that you do not loosen the underpinning.

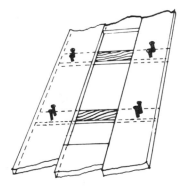

Screw 1"x2" pieces across the ends of the hole to be filled. Do not use nails to hold the 1x2's, because they will eventually lose their grip as people walk on the new board.

Refinishing Old Wood Floors

Any wood floor that is in reasonable condition can be refinished with relative ease as long as you are patient and willing to follow *all* the steps.

SANDING. You will need to rent two sanding machines—a large, heavy drum-type sander and a small, circular edging sander. Rentals are between $17 and $25 per day for both sanders, plus the cost of the sandpaper and floor finish.

The procedure for refinishing wood floors must be followed exactly.

1) Drive all loose nails beneath the floor surface.
2) Fill all small cracks between boards with wood putty.
3) Nail down all loose boards at the joists.
4) The first sanding is performed with the drum sander using coarse—3½ or 20—sandpaper, and should be done with the grain of the boards. The purpose of using coarse sandpaper is to grind down the floorboards until they are even. Start the sanding machine with the drum tilted up off the floor, then gradually bring the sandpaper down to the wood as you move the sander forward. Do not stop the machine while the drum is down, or the sandpaper will gouge the floor. Do the floor in drum-wide strips by first walking forward, then pulling the machine backward over the same path, overlapping each strip by approximately 3″. Before

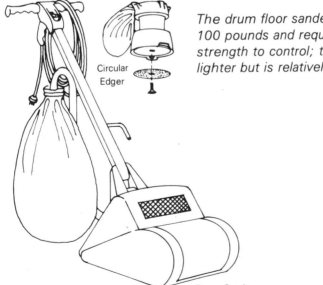

Circular Edger

The drum floor sander weighs about 100 pounds and requires considerable strength to control; the edger is lighter but is relatively as powerful.

Drum Sander

you turn off the machine, tip it back to elevate the paper from the wood, and hold it there until the drum has stopped rotating.

5) When you have sanded as much of the floor as you can with the drum sander, use the circular edger with coarse (3½ or 20) sandpaper to get at all of the areas along the baseboards missed by the big machine.

Caution: Both the drum and circular sander are heavy, powerful machines. Keep a firm grip on them when they are running, or they will literally propel themselves through the nearest wall.

6) Sweep up all the sawdust left from the first sanding. Sand the floor with the drum sander, using a medium-grit paper — 1½ or 40. Then do the edges with a medium-grit paper on the edger.

7) Sweep up your sawdust and put fine-grit — 2/0 or 100 — paper on the machines. The floor may *feel* smooth after its second sanding, but it is not. It is absolutely essential that the wood be smoothed with fine paper. Sand the floor with the drum sander and complete your finish sanding with the edger.

8) Remove all dust from the floor, window ledges, the tops of the baseboards — everywhere — with a vacuum cleaner. Then damp-mop the floor. Any dust left anywhere in the room is liable to settle on the finish material while it is drying and make the floor rough.

STAINING.   If the sanded floor is to be stained, the stain should be applied as soon as the floor is sanded smooth and cleaned. Allow the stain to dry for at least 12 hours.

APPLYING SANDER-FILLER.   Wood is an uneven material and in any floor there will be boards or parts of boards that soak up the finish material more than others, leaving what appear to be dry or unglossy spots. Although applying a sander-filler is not an absolutely necessary step, it will usually reduce the number of finish coats needed. The sander-filler fills in the spaces between the wood fibers and is applied after the stain is dry. If the floor feels rough after the filler dries (in about six hours), give the wood a hand sanding with fine-grit paper.

APPLYING POLYURETHANE. These days, practically everyone uses polyurethane varnish as a floor finish. If you have applied a coat of sander-filler as an undercoat, you probably will not need more than two coats of polyurethane. The first coat may be applied with either a paint roller or brush and will need about 12 hours to dry. The second coat should be put on with a brush in the same way you would apply any varnish (see page 103). If two coats of polyurethane do not produce the desired gloss or leave the floor rough, hand-sand the floor with fine-grit paper and apply a third and, if necessary, a fourth coat.

Finishing New Floors

The procedure for finishing a newly laid floor is precisely the same as followed for old floors. However, if the underlayment is firm and the new wood is even, the sanding can be confined to the medium-grit stage followed by the fine-grit stage. If the floor is in any way uneven, start with the coarse-grit stage to grind the boards down so they are level.

Resilient Flooring

Resilient flooring is available both in squares (usually 12"x12" or 9"x9") and as sheet goods that come in 6' and 12' widths and almost any length. There is a wide range of both sheet goods and tiles made from a variety of materials; each type requires a slightly different installation procedure. Easy instructions for laying a particular type of resilient floor usually come with the material and should be followed exactly.

Both sheet goods and tiles must be laid on an even, smooth surface — something that is not always provided by the floor itself.

Consequently, you may have to nail an underlayment to the floor before you can install the resilient flooring. On a relatively even floor, you can use ⅛" or ¼" hardboard. If the floor is uneven, choose ½" or thicker plywood. Screw-type nails should be used to fasten underlayment, placed 2" to 3" apart along the edges, 3" to 4" apart where pieces butt and 6" to 8" apart elsewhere. When you are finished there should not be any springiness in the under-layment, and no nailheads should protrude above its surface.

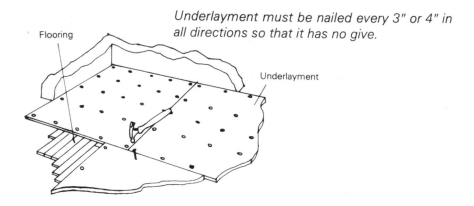

Underlayment must be nailed every 3" or 4" in all directions so that it has no give.

Flooring

Underlayment

Repairing Resilient Floors

Minor problems can arise with a resilient floor that has been in use for several years, so the repair of either the flooring or its underlayment may be necessary.

BUCKLING. Large bulges in a resilient floor are most likely caused by humidity which has expanded the underlayment. You will have to begin by cutting away enough of the flooring so that all of the affected area is exposed.

Use your hammer and chisel to remove the damaged under-layment, then nail in its place a patch of whatever underlayment material was used. Nail the patch tightly; nails should be 2" apart around the edges and 4″ apart in all directions across the face of the patch. Replace the flooring material with the appropriate adhesive, or cement a new patch in place.

DAMAGED TILES.   Tiles are normally bonded to floors with an adhesive. Should a tile become damaged or need replacing, begin by applying heat to it with a warm iron. When the adhesive is sufficiently softened, pry the tile up with the blade of your putty knife and peel it off the floor. If the tile still won't come off, you will have to use a hammer and chisel to chip it away. Always work from the center out to the edges so that you don't damage the corners of the surrounding tiles.

When the tile is completely removed, scrape all the remaining adhesive off the subflooring. Then position the replacement tile over the hole. If the tile must be trimmed, use a straightedge and utility knife to cut the edges to size. Next apply adhesive, generally known as mastic, to the underlayment and warm the new tile with an iron until it is flexible. Insert the new tile on the adhesive and weight it down for as long as it takes the adhesive to dry. The drying time varies from one to six hours depending on the product used.

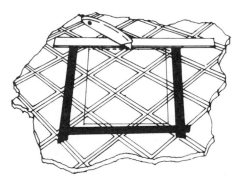

When replacing a damaged part of resilient flooring, tape your patch over the old flooring and cut through both old and new material at the same time so that the patch will fit exactly.

CURLED TILES. Sometimes a tile will curl up at its corners even when it has been properly installed. To repair a curled tile, first heat the corner with a moderately warm iron to soften the adhesive. Then pull the tile back far enough so that you can apply more adhesive. Replace the tile and weight it down until the adhesive is dry.

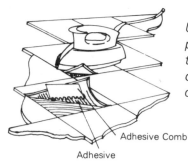

Use a warm iron to soften the mastic; peel back curled resilient flooring enough to apply new adhesive with an adhesive comb. Replace the square and weight it down until the new mastic is dry.

Adhesive Comb

Adhesive

PATCHING SHEET FLOORING. Worn or damaged sections of sheet flooring can be repaired by placing a piece of the same material over the damaged area so that it matches the surrounding pattern. Using a straightedge and utility knife, cut through both the new patch and the damaged flooring, and remove the cut area in the flooring. Clean all the adhesive from the underlayment and apply adhesive to the back of the patch. The patch should fit exactly into the hole; weight it down until the adhesive is dry.

REMOVING STAINS. Stains that appear on resilient flooring can be removed by rubbing them with one of the following: household bleach, white vinegar and water, hydrogen peroxide, rubbing alcohol, ammonia, lighter fluid or nail polish remover. If the stain covers the entire floor and is sticky, it is probably the result of wax buildup and can be removed with a strong ammonia solution or commercial cleaner.

STAIRS

Every staircase is made up of two pieces of wood called *stringers* which angle between floors and support a series of evenly spaced steps between them. There are two types of stair construction: open stringer and closed stringer. The *open-stringer* type has notches in the top edge of one or both stringers so that the horizontal *treads* and vertical *risers* that make up each step can be positioned over the edges of the notches. The

Anatomy of a stairway.

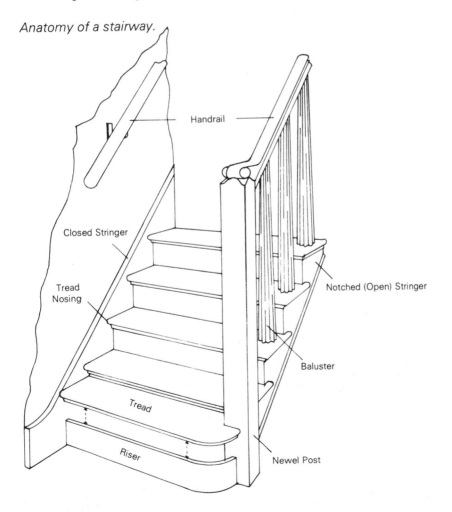

Handrail

Closed Stringer

Tread
Nosing

Notched (Open) Stringer

Baluster

Tread

Riser

Newel Post

closed-stringer construction has stringers with straight edges and grooves (mortises) cut into their inside faces to hold the treads and risers.

Many staircases are a combination of the two construction types, with the closed stringer positioned against a wall and the other stringer allowing the outside edges of the steps to hang over the stringer notches.

The visible parts of a stair include the stringers, the vertical riser, the horizontal tread and molding under the lip of each tread. The unseen parts include nails, glue, the grooves in a closed stringer, and the triangular glue blocks that may be behind the joints between the tread and the riser. There may also be wedges driven into the closed-stringer mortises to give the joint stability.

If a staircase has at least one open side, all repairs can be made from above. But the only way to repair a closed-stringer assembly is from underneath the stairs. Moreover, if the closed-stringer stairway has additional supports under it, the replacement of a single step becomes a major repair job.

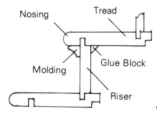

Side view of a step and how it is put together.

Repairing Squeaks

REPAIRING FROM ABOVE. This can be done by toenailing screw-type nails into the riser through the top front edge of the tread. If the squeak comes from the back of a tread, you may be able to drive small wedges between the riser and the top of the offending tread. The ends of the wedges are then cut off with a utility saw or a knife.

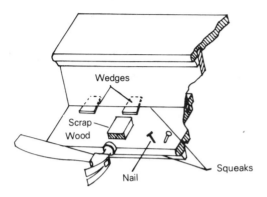

Squeaky stairs can be repaired by toenailing nails into the riser. Or, if the squeak is at the back of the step, you can drive wedges under the rear riser.

REPAIRING FROM BELOW. Provided the back of the stairs can be reached, this is done in any of three ways. 1) You can glue and screw blocks along the joint between the tread and the riser. 2) You can screw metal brackets to the back of the riser and underside of the tread. 3) You can drive wedges up into the mortise on the underside of the front of the tread.

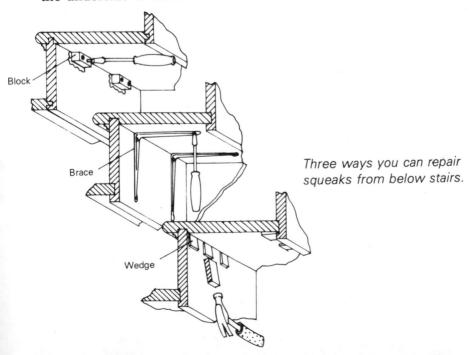

Three ways you can repair squeaks from below stairs.

Replacing Stairs

REPLACING FROM ABOVE.   This is never a simple repair job and is done only when the back of the staircase is inaccessible. Well-constructed stairs are mortised so that the riser fits into slots in the treads above and below it. The riser itself may be beveled to fit against the stringer, and be rabbetted at both its top and bottom. You can cut the bevels in a replacement tread or riser with your saber saw and rout out the mortises and rabbets with a hammer, chisel and plane. But the time and effort you will have to expend makes it more feasible to hire a professional carpenter with the right power tools to do the job, particularly if more than one stair needs replacement.

REPLACING FROM BELOW.   This is not as complicated, pro-vided you have access to the back of the staircase. If the stairs are in a closed-stringer unit, they have been assembled in mortises and there are probably glue blocks under the treads. The back of the staircase may be covered with lath and plaster, hardboard or sheetrock and may have vertical supports, all of which must be removed before the following procedure for replacing the tread and riser can begin.

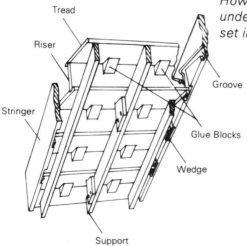

How an open stairway looks from underneath. The steps and risers are set in mortises cut in both stringers.

Tread

Riser

Groove

Stringer

Glue Blocks

Wedge

Support

1) Work carefully with a hammer and chisel to remove the wedges supporting the tread and riser in their mortises. The wedges are normally both glued and nailed, so you will have to break them apart.

2) If the tread and riser are not mortised together, the riser can now be pulled down, away from the tread. There may be ·nails or screws holding the pieces together, and these must either be cut with a hacksaw or otherwise removed.

3) If the tread and riser are mortised together, drill a hole through the riser at the edge of the tread and use a utility saw to cut the riser, then pull it down out of its slots.

4) From the front of the stairs, use a hammer to tap the tread toward the back of the stringers until it slides out of its grooves.

5) Insert the new tread and riser into the stringer mortises and drive new wedges behind them. The wedges should be coated with glue and pounded into the mortises until the tread and riser fit tightly in place. The riser and tread can be nailed or, better still, fastened along their joint with screws placed every 6″.

Five steps in replacing a stair from below.

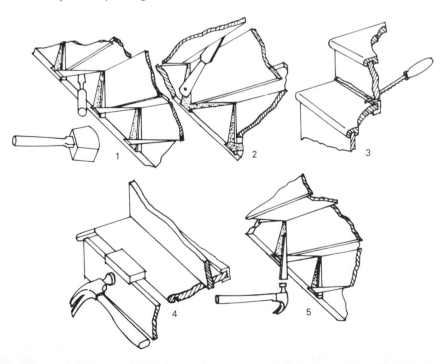

Loose Balusters

The *balusters* that support most railings are fitted into angled slots in the edge of each stair and their tops are fitted into holes in the underside of the *handrail. Balustrades,* which consist of a handrail, baluster and newel post, are commonly made of hardwood, which means the wood may split if you drive any nails or screws into it without first drilling pilot holes.

Balusters that are loose at the top (under the handrail) can be secured by driving wedges coated with glue either into the hole in the handrail or between the top of the baluster and the handrail. An alternative is to drill a pilot hole diagonally up through the top of the baluster and into the handrail, then countersink a long flathead screw through the two units.

If the baluster is loose at the bottom, examine the molding attached to the edge of the stair to be sure it is absolutely tight. If the molding is loose, tighten it. The slots that hold the balusters are flanged to hold the baluster firmly, but the baluster is not glued or otherwise secured, so the wood is free to expand and contract during weather changes. The flanged slot can be filled by driving wedges around the base of the baluster. Screws can also be driven through the tenon of the baluster and into the stair tread, provided you first drill pilot holes so the wood does not split.

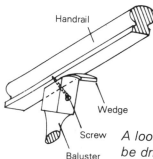

Handrail

Wedge

Screw

Baluster

A loose baluster can be wedged, or a screw may be driven upward at an angle into the handrail.

SIX

The Care and Preening of Walls and Ceilings

NONE OF THE REPAIRS YOU WILL HAVE TO MAKE ON the faces of walls or ceilings are very difficult, but they do require buying special materials which must be used with considerable patience.

Before you attack any wall or ceiling, determine how it was constructed and exactly where the joists or studs were placed. The most important fact to remember about both joists and studs is that they are supposed to be spaced either 16″ or 24″ on center. "On center" means that the distance between each member is exactly 16″ or 24″ from the center of one member to the center of the next member.

At any point where two walls intersect, the connection probably was made by nailing three 2″x4″ studs together in such a way that there are nailing surfaces for all inside and outside surfaces of the wall. In buildings built prior to World War II the members are likely to be bridged by a series of thin wooden strips called *lath,* with spaces left between each strip to hold the plaster of paris that makes up the face of the wall or ceiling. Since World War II, the usual method of covering studs and joists has been to nail drywall panels (also called wallboard, gypsumboard, sheet-

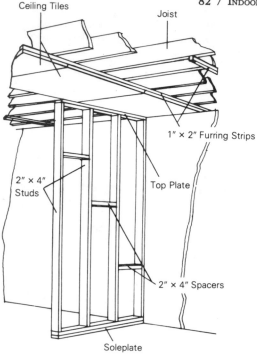

How walls and ceilings are framed.

rock or plasterboard) to the studs. These panels are preferable to plaster because they are quicker and cheaper to assemble and easier to repair or replace.

THE TROUBLE WITH WALLS

There is one thing to remember about every wall in every dwelling: it can't be trusted. Hang your combination square from a string tacked near the corner of any wall and if the string absolutely parallels the corner in both directions, enshrine the corner and charge admission to the millions of housebuilders who will want to come and ogle it.

Houses continually shift, and there can be infinitesimal mistakes made in the carpentry and/or plastering of every wall, so they are almost never absolutely vertical. Measure the length of any wall from corner to corner at the ceiling; and then measure it again at the floor, and you will almost always have two different distances to contend with. So never trust a wall, and never use a corner as the starting point for any accurate calculations.

Finding Wall Studs

There is another little indiscretion about walls. In theory you should be able to measure either 16" or 24" out from any corner, drive a nail into the wall, and strike the solid wood of a stud. But it is astounding how few walls offer up the location of their studs so easily. In fact, locating studs can become quite a frustrating experience.

You have to find the studs in a wall anytime you want to hang a heavy mirror or bookshelves, or if you want to place an electrical box or install a doorway. There are several possible ways of finding studs:

1) The classic method is to tap along the wall with a hammer. When the tapping sounds solid rather than hollow, it is probably because you have located a stud. Drive a small nail into the spot and see if you strike wood. Once one stud is located, measuring 16" or 24" in either direction *ought* to locate the others.

2) Examine the baseboard closely. Often it is nailed to the bottoms of the studs, so any visible nailheads may indicate stud locations.

3) With wallboard, scrutinize the surface closely under the light of a bare bulb. Many times there are slight indentations over the nails used to secure wallboard panels to the studs. Once a stud

has been more or less located, take a small finishing nail or your drill and bore into the wall at 1″ intervals until you encounter solid wood. The small holes can be filled with joint compound.

4) If all else fails, pry the baseboard away from the wall and all of the wall's innermost secrets will be revealed to you. If you cannot actually see the studs, there will be plenty of visible nail-heads to tell you where they are.

Replacing Damaged Baseboard

When replacing a section of damaged baseboard, first pry the *shoe molding* away from the board, then pull it up from the floor. Now work your way slowly along the baseboard, driving a chisel between the board and the wall at regular intervals and prying the board outward. When you have removed the board from the wall, use it as a template to measure the replacement baseboard and determine where and how it must be cut. Remove all the nails protruding from the wall and place the new baseboard in position. Nail it at the studs and replace the shoe molding.

When the floor is uneven, rest the replacement baseboard along the wall in the exact position it will be placed. Measure the widest space between the floor and the bottom of the board and cut a small block of wood that is slightly thicker than the gap.

Anatomy of a baseboard and shoe molding.

After you have inscribed the bottom of the baseboard, cut along your line with a saber saw.

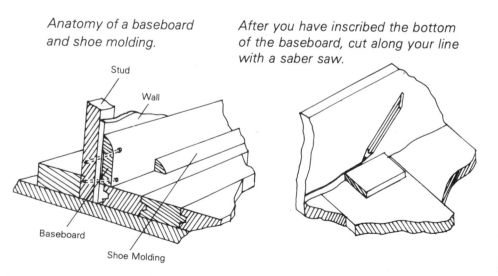

Stud

Wall

Baseboard

Shoe Molding

Hold a pencil to the top of the wood and slide the block along the floor next to the baseboard, marking the board. Now use your saber saw to cut the bottom of the baseboard along your scribed line. Position the baseboard against the wall and press it down against the floor as you nail it to the soleplate of the wall.

Drywall

Drywall, or wallboard, comes in $\frac{3}{8}''$, $\frac{1}{2}''$ and $\frac{5}{8}''$ thicknesses, in large sheets that range from 4'x6' to 4'x16', allowing a single panel to reach from the floor to the ceiling of rooms in most buildings. The panels consist of gypsum plaster compressed between two sheets of tough paper, so the panels are heavy but have no real strength of their own. As a result, they are always nailed into the framing of the house, or against some kind of wooden frame made with 2x4's, 2x3's or 1"x2" furring strips. The 1x2's are used when the panels are attached to an already existing wall or ceiling.

There is also a waterproof type of wallboard that is always $\frac{1}{2}''$ thick and colored green (because of the chemicals used to treat the paper). This type is normally used in bathrooms, behind kitchen sinks or wherever moisture might get at the wall. Aside from its color, the material is no different from any other wallboard.

As a rule, $\frac{5}{8}''$-thick wallboard is used on walls. The $\frac{1}{2}''$ thickness is recommended for ceilings, primarily because the thicker sheets are so heavy that they will, in time, loosen the nails that hold them in place.

The great advantage to wallboard is that you can cut it with a kitchen knife, razor blade, saber saw, utility knife — practically anything sharp. Although either side of a panel can be cut, the recommended procedure is to lay the panel on the floor with its good side down. The good side is pure white; the back is greyish. Using a straightedge, draw a line where you intend to cut. Then hold your straightedge against the line and use it as a guide for your knife. It is necessary to sever only the paper skin of the panel, but to do this you may have to draw the point of the knife along your line several times. When the paper has been cut, stand the panel on edge and bend it away from your cut. The plaster will break neatly along the cut and the pieces will fold back against each other, attached by the paper on the uncut side. Now insert the blade of your knife under the fold and pull it upward along the cut, severing the panel.

If the wallboard is already attached to a wall or ceiling and you want to cut a hole in it for, say, an electrical box or light fixture, first mark the outline of the hole. Then drill or punch a ¼" hole at one corner and use your saber saw to cut out the outline. Since you cannot be certain where pipes or wires are lurking behind the wall, use the shortest blade you own and work the saw very slowly. Stop if the blade meets any resistance and investigate what you are cutting into.

If an entire panel of wallboard must be replaced, first pull the old board off the wall, then remove all the nails left in the studs. Next, cut a new piece of board to fit into the hole and stand it up against the studs. Nail it along its edges, as well as anywhere the studs provide a backing.

Large-headed, cement-coated wallboard nails, annular ring nails or drywall Phillips-head screws can be used to hold wallboard in place. Start nailing down the center of the panel and work outward, spacing your nails every 6" or so. Nails should

Utility Saw

Holes in drywall can be cut with a knife, saber saw or utility saw.

never be closer than ⅜" from the edge of a panel and every nail should be "dimpled"—that is, driven deep enough into the panel so that the hammer head leaves the nailhead inside a round dent, but does not tear the paper facing of the wallboard. It is this dimple that allows you to bury the nail under joint compound so it never will be seen.

Concealing Joints and Nails

As soon as the wallboard panels are nailed, their joints and nailheads can be concealed. The adhesive recommended by wallboard manufacturers is wallboard joint compound. It can be purchased in one-gallon and five-gallon cans at most lumberyards where drywall panels are sold. The compound has a puttylike consistency, is ready to use and dries to an almost smooth texture that requires a minimum of hand sanding. The tape is made of a tough paper 2" wide, and is sold in perforated or non-perforated rolls 75', 250' or 500' long. It does not matter which type of tape you use.

The key to proper concealment of wallboard joints and nails is: never try to cover them with a single application of joint compound. Be prepared to put on at least two, and probably three, layers.

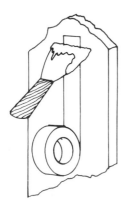

When applying wallboard tape, press it firmly against the wall with the blade of your taping knife held at almost a right angle to the tape.

Use your 4"-wide taping knife to apply a thick coat of joint compound the full length of both sides of the joint, and press the tape to the compound so that the tape spans the joint. Now draw your knife blade down the center of the tape, pushing it as hard as possible against the panel. The compound will ooze out from under the edges of the tape. Scrape it off the wall with your knife and put it back in its container for reuse. If properly done, the face of the tape should be pretty much dry and flat against the wallboard, and the compound around the edges should be barely noticeable.

The compound needs about 12 hours to dry, so forget it for a day. While it dries you can also wipe compound into the dimples around each nailhead, then scrape off all the excess on the surface of the panel (or you can put a patch of tape over the nailheads, but in most cases the tape is not necessary). When the first coat of compound dries over the nails it will sink, so there will have to be another coating.

The second layer of compound is slapped over the tape in globs and then scraped off until the compound barely covers the paper. It should extend approximately 2" beyond each side of the tape, where it will be feathered off against the panel. The nailheads also receive a second coating, which should extend out beyond the holes.

Each application of wallboard compound is begun by smearing plenty of compound over the area, then scraping most of it off. It is better to use several thin coats of compound than to try and cover a joint in one application.

Allow the compound time to dry completely before you apply a third coat. At this point you can feather out as much as 8″ on either side of the tape, trying to make it as smooth as possible. If the nailhead indentations still show, give them a third coating of compound and feather it out beyond the holes.

When the compound is thoroughly dry, hand-sand it with a medium- or fine-grit abrasive. Joint compound smoothes so easily that this procedure becomes nothing more than wiping the compound with abrasive, even when you are sanding down high ridges. But the sanding may reveal gouges in the compound that were not filled; give them a coat of compound.

Taping Corners — Inside and Out

To tape either inside or outside corners, follow the same procedure used to cover any wallboard joint. No matter which kind of tape you are using, it can be folded along the score that extends down its center and is then pushed into, or wrapped around, the corner. The working of the compound into an inside corner is slightly more difficult with a normal taping knife, since the edge of the knife tends to scrape whichever side has been coated first. You can buy an angled finishing knife, which is designed for corners, anywhere the tape and compound are sold.

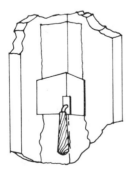

You can buy an angled corner-taping blade for under $2.

Repairing Wallboard

DENTS.   Dents and even small cracks that appear in wallboard can almost always be repaired simply by filling them with joint compound. The damaged area should be sanded with a rough abrasive to provide a grip for the compound, which is then applied in as many layers as necessary. When the compound is completely dry, sand it smooth.

DAMAGED TAPE.   Carefully pull the tape off the wall so that none of the face paper of the wallboard comes with it. Roughen the damaged area with an abrasive, apply compound and new tape, then add enough layers of compound to hide the area and make it even with the rest of the wall.

FILLING LARGE HOLES.   This is a more complicated repair problem. Whenever possible, cut out a section of the wallboard around the damaged area that is long enough to reach between at least two studs. Then cut a piece of wallboard to fit in the hole and nail it to the studs. The joints around the piece must, of course, be compounded and taped.

If you cannot fix the damage in the above manner, cut a square of scrap wallboard larger than the damaged area. Hold the scrap over the hole and trace its outline on the wall, then cut out a hole along the outline. Also cut a scrap piece of wood that is narrower than the hole and at least 4″ longer than the hole is wide. Coat both ends of the board with white or cream glue. Position it behind the hole and clamp it to the edges with C-clamps, then

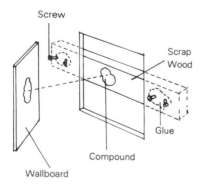

When attaching a backup board behind a hole in your wall, use screws to hold it in place, then glue it with wallboard compound.

drill pilot holes for screws through the wallboard into both ends of the wood and screw the wood in place. Now apply joint compound to the exposed front of the wood and along the edges of the patch. Insert the patch in the hole against the wooden backstop and prop a piece of wood (or something heavy) against it until the compound dries. Then tape and compound the edges of the patch.

Nailing Wallboard to Brick

When a brick wall is to be covered by wallboard, first nail 1"x2" furring strips to the brick, using masonry nails or lead plugs and screws. The vertical strips should be placed at least every 24", with horizontal strips across the top and bottom of the wall. Then nail the wallboard to the furring.

Patching Plaster Walls

Plaster walls develop both hairline and large cracks caused by settlement, vibration, changes in the weather and, most likely, old age. In most instances the crack, or dent or small hole, can be filled with a patching material such as spackle, plaster of paris or joint compound. Whatever material is used, the procedure is the same.

1) Always remove any loose particles around the damaged area. If the damage is a crack, use a hooked or pointed tool (such as an old-fashioned can opener) to gouge out the crack and enlarge it enough to angle its edges inward and provide a better grip for the filler material.

2) If the patching material is plaster of paris or spackle, the area to be filled must be thoroughly dampened before the filler is applied so that it will adhere properly. If joint compound is used, apply it only to a dry, clean area. Press the patching material tightly into the crack or hole and wipe away any excess, then allow the filler to dry completely (you may have to wait at least 12 hours).

3) Shrinkage may occur during the drying period, causing the filler to crack or sink. If this happens, simply apply a second layer and allow it to dry before you sand the patch and apply a coat of primer paint.

If a large hole in a plaster wall is deep enough to expose wooden lath, bear in mind that the lath is probably very old and therefore extremely dry. Even if the wood is thoroughly dampened first, it will quickly draw too much moisture from any filler material that comes into contact with it, reducing the strength of the filler. The best way to avoid this particular problem is to fill the hole with pieces of wallboard or bend a piece of metal mesh around the lath. Then apply filler. If you fill the hole with scraps of wallboard, the job can be finished off with joint compound. With the metal mesh, you have to mix spackle with a little plaster of paris and apply it to the metal in two applications. The mesh should be dampened and the first layer of filler pressed hard against it so that it is forced into the holes in the mesh. When the first coat is dry, apply a second layer and scrape away any excess plaster or spackle. When that is dry, sand the area smooth and prime it.

If the lath behind a smaller hole is broken, stuff the hole with newspaper so that the filler will have some sort of backing. If the hole is too large for the newspaper method, insert a piece of wire mesh behind the hole and wire it tightly to a stick that spans the front of the hole and holds the mesh in place. Apply the first layer of filler and allow it to dry before removing the stick. Then add the final layer of filler.

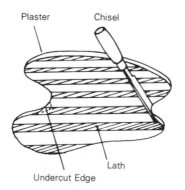

Plaster   Chisel

Lath

Undercut Edge

Use a chisel to undercut the edges of a plaster hole to provide a better grip for whatever patching material you are using.

The pencil or stick is left holding the wire mesh until after the first coat of plaster has dried. Remove the pencil before applying your finish coat.

COVERING CEILINGS

Nailing wallboard to a ceiling is hard to do alone, particularly if entire panels are being placed. Even with two men holding a panel against the ceiling, it takes muscle until the first half-dozen nails are placed and can hold it in position. Many professionals build a T-brace by nailing a 4'-long board across the end of a 2x4 cut to the exact height of the ceiling. The panel is then lifted into place and braced against the ceiling by one or two T-braces. At that point, you can nail without the added strain of holding up the panel.

PANELING

In recent years paneling manufacturers have increased the variety of paneling that can be used to cover a wall, a ceiling, an entire room. Most paneling comes in 4'x8' sheets and in thicknesses ranging from ⅛" to 7/16"; generally the thicker the sheet, the better its quality and durability. Paneling is made from a variety of materials, beginning with real wood. Then there are hardwood panels that have a plastic facing, gypsumboard panels, softwood panels and planks and pure plastic laminates. The cost of paneling ranges from $5 to $100 a sheet, but no matter what you buy it can be installed with nails, glue or both. In some cases, such as on masonry or plaster walls that are uneven or crumbling, the panels must be mounted on a gridwork of 1″x2″ furring strips; manufacturers provide specific installation instructions which should be followed closely. Here are a few tips for making the job of installing panels a little easier:

1) Remove all moldings and trim in the room before putting up any paneling.

2) Locate all wall studs and plan your job around them. Cut the first panel so that its edge falls on a stud near a corner, then install the other panels so that no panel will be less than 6″ wide.

3) Rather than cutting pieces to fit around a window or door opening, place the panel over the opening, tack it in place with three or four nails, drill a pilot hole for your saber saw, then cut out the excess. The window and door trim can be put back in place over the paneling.

4) To cut out sections of a panel for electrical outlets, smear lipstick on the edge of the outlet, then press the panel in place. The imprint of the outlet will be left on the back of the panel, ready for cutting out with either a utility or saber saw.

TILING

Ceramic tiles are available in an almost endless variety, and all are easy to install.

A *standard tile* measures 4¼″x4¼″x¼″ (although this can vary slightly) and comes in a huge variety of colors and shapes, plain or with fancy patterns. Generally the fancier the pattern, the more expensive the tile.

Ceramic tile can also be purchased in *sheet form* — 1'-square sheets with the tiles segmented into standard 4¼" squares. The sheet is installed with adhesive and then a grout is wiped over the tiles to fill the joints between the tile segments. Sheet tile also offers a range of colors and textures.

Ceramic tile in *mosaic form* consists of tiny (less than 1'-square each) shapes, which are mounted on a mesh backing that can be cut between the tiles to make installation easier. This type of tile also comes in various colors and patterns and is favored by most people for covering floors.

You will need to acquire two or three special tools if you plan to lay any tile, but none of them are expensive. A *toothed spreader* is used to spread the adhesive and can be any of several designs and sizes. When you apply the adhesive, spread it evenly over the floor or wall so that all the tiles will be level. For certain types of tile you may also need a *ceramic tile cutter,* but most dealers will either rent or loan it to you, and show you how to use it into the bargain. Finally, you will have to buy an inexpensive pair of *tile-cutting pliers* which are used for nibbling away small pieces of tile.

When planning a tile installation try to avoid cutting any more tiles than necessary or having a lot of small pieces to fit, especially where they will be noticeable, such as near the front of a tub or around a door or window.

Tiling the Walls Around a Bathtub

The first row of tiles should be set directly on the tub and checked with the level on your combination square. If the row is level, the tiles can be set. If the first row is not level, use your square to mark out a true line on all three walls to determine how far off the row is. If there will be a gap of more than ¼" between the tub and the tiles, trim the bottom of the tiles to fit on the low side. If the gap is less than ¼", use grout to fill in the space.

Unless the first row is level, you also have to draw intersecting level and plumb lines on all three walls around the tub as guides to tile placement. When you have determined where each tile will be placed, begin your installation wherever the level and plumb lines intersect. Butter the first tile with adhesive and place it exactly on the intersection.

All tiles have tiny nibs molded into their edges so that when they are butted together they automatically leave a space to be filled by grout. Once your first tile is in place you can spread adhesive all around it and accurately lay all the other tiles merely by butting them squarely against each other.

If small corners must be cut out of a tile — for example, to fit around a fixture — cut the tile all the way across the face in one direction, then the other. The unwanted corner can be discarded and the pieces you want are then reassembled on the wall.

The grout used to fill the spaces between tiles is sold in the form of a powder which is basically portland cement. The grout is mixed with water to about the consistency of putty and forced into the joints between the tiles, using either a squeegee, your hands or both. Grout can irritate your skin, so it is a good idea to wear rubber gloves. The excess is then wiped off the face of the tiles with a damp sponge and rags. There are different types of grout but each of them has instructions for mixing, applying and drying printed on their packages.

Split wall tiles whenever you have to cut off corners or go around a fixture, then reassemble the pieces on the wall.

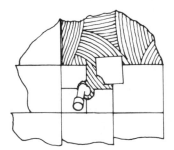

Laying a Tile Floor

Laying tiles on a floor is even easier than putting them on walls. However, tiles should be placed on an even surface, which means you will have to nail underlayment to an uneven floor (see page 72).

You want to cut as few tiles as possible, and those you do cut should be placed near the baseboards, as far from view as possible. It is wise to lay all the tiles down on the floor before you apply any adhesive. This will tell you exactly which tiles must be cut. You can also trace the position of the tiles closest to the center of the room with a pencil. Spread adhesive over the center portion of the room, using a saw-toothed trowel which leaves a series of ridges in the adhesive. This tool guarantees that you apply just the right amount of adhesive, and allows you to see enough of your pencil lines between ridges to guide your placement of the tiles. Now begin laying tiles at the outlines you traced on the floor. Then work out toward the walls.

If you are tiling a bathroom floor you may want to give the room a tile baseboard, which is installed after the floor is laid. Only when all the tiles are in place should the grout be applied.

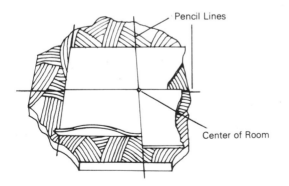

Pencil Lines

Center of Room

Begin laying floor tiles at the center of the room and work out toward the walls so that cut tiles will be less noticeable.

Bathroom Tile Repairs

Into every bathroom there will someday come a damaged tile that you will want to replace. To remove a tile, use a ¾" chisel and chip away at the corners. Then insert the chisel blade under the tile and hammer toward the center, prying it out. Use the chisel to scrape away all the adhesive left on the wall.

The new tile is installed with tile adhesive and grout, or by anchoring it in a bed of plaster of paris. If more than a few tiles are damaged or loose, part of the wall has probably given way. You will have to remove the affected portion of the wall and replace it with a piece of waterproof wallboard nailed to the wall studs. If the wall is plaster and lath, knock out the old plaster with your hammer and expose the studs, then install the wallboard. Filling holes in a plaster wall usually requires two layers of wallboard nailed together to bring the patch flush with the face of the surrounding plaster. Once the wallboard is in place, you can install your tiles as usual.

Another tile-related problem occurs when grout in the joint between the bottom row of tiles and the tub begins to crumble. Dig out all the loose, crumbly material with a screwdriver or other pointed tool, then apply silicone caulk. The caulk comes in tubes in various colors, and is applied in a bead along the joint, then pressed into the space with a taping knife or your finger. The same caulking, incidentally, can be used anywhere you find an unwanted opening between a kitchen or bathroom sink and its counter top.

SEVEN

Finishing Off — Paint and Wallcoverings

PAINTING

Choosing Paint

Finish paint can be divided into two basic types: *oil-base* and *water-base (latex)*. There is still a lot of debate over which is better, but most professionals lean toward the latex simply because it's soluble in water, which makes thinning and cleanup easy.

When you are buying paint, price is a good criterion of quality. A good *flat paint* — the kind used to cover walls and ceilings — will cost you at least $7 a gallon; *enamel,* which is used for kitchens, baths and woodwork, will cost $9 or $10 a gallon. Both enamel and *varnish* come in gloss or semigloss forms.

In addition to the flat and enamel paints, you can buy special paints for problem situations. *Texture paint,* for example, has a thin, jellylike consistency and is used for covering walls or ceilings that are riddled with small cracks or are otherwise in poor condition. Texture paint is expensive, however, comes in a limited number of colors, and removing it requires sanding with heavy-duty machines.

Sand paint is another special-purpose paint. Because it dries to a sandy, masonry-like finish, it is a good choice wherever old paint has peeled heavily. However, its hiding ability is not as great as that of texture paint.

Epoxy paint is used to cover bath fixtures, glass, plastic laminate and other nonporous objects. It comes in two cans whose contents are mixed together immediately before use. The epoxies are very expensive and you must be extremely careful to follow the instructions on the cans or the paint will not adhere properly.

Fire-resistant paint can be used in the same way as any interior paint and should be chosen for any area where fire is a particular hazard. It comes in standard colors.

Primers

Usually more than one coat of paint will be required for any paint job. If colors are being changed from a dark hue to a lighter one, or a previously unpainted surface is being covered, or a wall must be patched extensively, a prime coat must be applied under the finish paint. Primers seal the wall, make a smooth surface for the finish paint and provide "tooth" for the finish paint to grip.

Enamel undercoater is used on bare wood or metal that is to be painted with a gloss or semigloss enamel. *Alkyd primer-sealer* is for new dry plaster as well as for plaster that has been previously painted. *Latex primer-sealer* may be used on raw drywall or on plaster that is new or old. If a new wood is to be stained, a pigmented *shellac primer* should be used.

Tools

You will need some special tools for painting interior surfaces. If you plan to cover walls and ceilings with a flat paint,

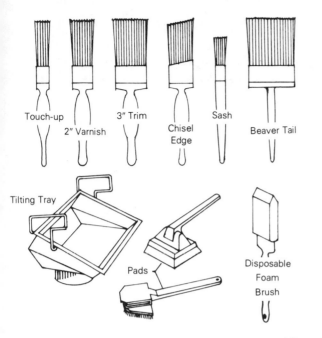

Brushes and painting pads used in house painting.

Touch-up

2" Varnish

3" Trim

Chisel Edge

Sash

Beaver Tail

Tilting Tray

Pads

Disposable Foam Brush

nothing beats a *roller*. These come in 7" and 9" lengths with naps of various lengths. A short-nap roller is best for applying flat paint. Don't buy a roller that has seams showing or that bends when squeezed. You would also be wise to get the kind of handle that allows the roller to be slid on and off, rather than the type with wing nuts.

There are many kinds of paintbrushes available, but they can be divided into two basic types: those with synthetic fibers (such as nylon) and those with natural bristles (such as hog's hair).

For house painting, you will require a few nylon brushes: a 2", 2½" or 3" brush for cutting in where the roller cannot go and for painting narrow woodwork and trim (windows, molding); and a 4" brush for larger woodwork (doors). When painting or particularly when varnishing furniture, always use a brush with natural bristles. Never use a natural-bristle brush with any water-base paint—the bristles will become waterlogged and soggy.

Each type of brush has its own particular use. The long-handled *sash and trim brushes* are meant to be gripped as if you were holding a pencil, and are used for cutting in and to cover woodwork and molding. When it comes to painting a whole wall, you will need a wider, heavier *beaver tail brush,* which has a stout handle that is most comfortably held as if it were a tennis racquet. Then there are the *chisel-edged brushes* which are held with your thumb on one side and your fingers on the other, and are designed for beading.

You can also find painting kits on the market that consist of several kinds of foam rubber painting pads and brushes. If you have the opportunity to buy a set (they cost around $8), do it. In the hands of neophyte or professional, they do a remarkable job of putting paint on walls and woodwork smoothly, and in very short order. The best part of the foam rubber applicators is that they leave no brush strokes.

Basics of Brush Work

Before you use any new brush, hold it under running water and tug at the bristles to get rid of all the loose ones, which might get stuck on your project. With that chore accomplished, you are ready to begin painting.

Never dip any more than half the length of the bristles in the paint and never wipe the bristles against the side of the paint can. The correct way of getting excess paint off a brush is to tap the metal ferrule of the brush on the rim of the can. Each brush stroke should be about twice the length of the bristles of your brush, and you need to exert very little pressure on the bristles. Work in small sections, covering the area with short, overlapping strokes. As you start each new section, begin about two brush lengths away from a completed one and work toward the wet paint.

CUTTING IN. This is the act of painting a strip roughly 2″ wide down the corner of a room and is usually done prior to painting the rest of the wall with a roller. When you are cutting in, you can start anywhere by taking half a dozen overlapping brush strokes perpendicular to the edge of the wall; then smooth the paint with a single long stroke. Work your way up the full height of the wall in this manner, then finish off with one last, wall-length stroke.

BEADING. This takes a little practice and must be done with a chisel-edged brush. Believe it or not, without much practice you can achieve a steady, straight edge anywhere you want two colors to meet, or even paint the narrow dividers between windowpanes without the need of masking tape. If you press the bristles of a chisel-edged brush flat against the painting surface, you can force a thin line of paint (the bead) about $\frac{1}{16}''$ from the edge of the surface you want the paint to meet. The wet paint will spread out enough to reach the line you want drawn.

WINDOWS AND BASEBOARDS. Even before you master the technique of beading, there is one secret to painting windows: don't be afraid of them. If paint gets on the glass, wipe it off immediately with a rag dipped in whatever solvent you are using with the paint.

There is also a technique for painting baseboards so that you avoid dripping paint on the floor. The procedure is to dip the brush halfway into the paint, tap it on the inside of the can, then apply paint to the *middle* of the baseboard. Next paint the top and, finally, cover the area near the floor with an undipped brush (to minimize the chance of getting paint on the floorboards).

ENAMEL AND VARNISH. Enamel is really varnish with a pigment, so you can safely use the same techniques when applying either. You should load your brush a little more than you would with a flat paint and flow material on the surface, using longer strokes. Do not go back over your work any more than is absolutely necessary, and try not to bend the bristles of the brush any more than you have to. As soon as your brush begins to need a refill, cross-stroke your work at right angles to the original direction, using a feather-light touch and very little paint on the tip of the brush. The object here is to fill in the ridges left by the brush and provide a smooth finish.

Roller Work

Roller work requires no special preparation or training. You pour paint into the roller pan, roll the roller through the paint and go to work. Your first stroke should be upward and should be about 3' long. Then, without lifting the roller from the surface, make a "W" roughly 3' square and fill in the area by crisscrossing strokes. There is no need to finish the section with strokes all going the same direction. Simply move on to cover the next 3' square.

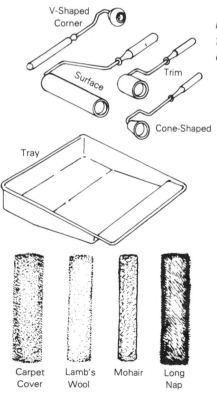

Paint rollers come in various shapes for painting different areas. Different covers are also available.

Preparation

The key to achieving a good paint job is in thoroughly preparing the surface to be painted. This means that all holes and cracks must be patched and sanded smooth.

Before the finish paint is applied over any patch, the patch should be primed. Allow the primer to dry completely before finish-painting, or the patch will show through the paint. Primed plasterboard patches should be fine-sanded to prevent the paper covering from becoming fuzzy; if the top coat of paint is to be enamel, your primer should be (or contain) shellac. When buying the shellac, be sure it is labeled "three-pound cut" so that your base is the proper strength.

To save yourself energy during a job, first move all the furniture out of your way and cover it with an inexpensive plastic sheet.

Painting a Room

Always start painting a room in the darkest corner of the ceiling and work toward the light source, so that you can readily see your "holidays," or missed spots. Use a 2″ brush to cut in the joint where the ceiling meets the walls. Then fill in the ceiling, using a roller. Use plenty of paint on the roller to prevent hard rolling and poor coverage, and always work in small, 3′ squares.

Walls are also painted in 3′ squares. Start at a corner by cutting in a 3′-long strip from the top of the wall (about a third of the way down the corner) with a brush. Fill in the area with a roller, then continue along the wall, filling in corresponding 3′ squares. If enamel is to be used on the woodwork, wait until the wall paint is dry, then do the entire baseboard, and the door and window moldings.

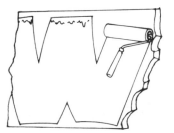

When rolling paint on a wall, work in 3′-square areas.

WALLCOVERINGS

Twenty or 25 years ago when people referred to wallpaper, they meant just that—paper with colored designs on it to be put on walls. Today, the term is applicable to a wide variety of coverings that are more accurately called wallcoverings. They include the old-fashioned wallpaper, vinyl-coated paper and vinyl-coated fabric. There are also vinyl self-stick sheets that have an adhesive backing, as well as foil and flock, which feels like damask or velvet. All of these come in rolls about 27" wide and 15' long, but lengths and widths can vary.

Tools and Equipment

In order to hang wallcovering that requires paste, you must buy some special tools, either separately or in a kit. The kit costs about $10 and includes a large *paste brush*, short-bristled

The equipment needed for hanging wallcoverings.

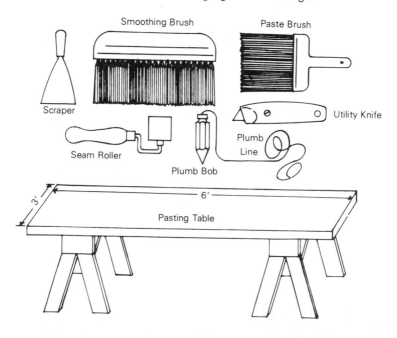

Smoothing Brush

Paste Brush

Scraper

Utility Knife

Seam Roller

Plumb Line

Plumb Bob

6'

3'

Pasting Table

smoothing brush, seam roller and single-edge razor-blade *trimming knife.* Aside from these tools, it is necessary to have a piece of string attached to a light weight (such as scissors) to use as a *plumb line,* perhaps a *paint scraper,* a *pail* to mix the paste in and a long *pasting table* to work on.

Preparation

The walls to be covered should be in sound condition. Repair all cracks and holes. If the wall has any enamel on it, wash the paint with ammonia to remove its gloss and roughen the surface enough to aid the adhesion of the paste. If the wall already has paper on it and both are in sound condition, you can put the new paper right on top. But if the old paper is in bad condition it must come off, which probably means the rental of a wallpaper steamer and definitely forbodes a lot of long, messy work. The process of removal begins by scratching the paper with rough sandpaper. Then steam is applied which seeps through the scratches to the paste and softens it, allowing you to scrape off the paper.

Covering Walls

Follow this procedure:

1) Measure the width of the wallcovering. Subtract 1" from this measurement and hang a plumb line that distance from the edge of a door or window (*not* a corner). You can tack the plumb line to the crown molding along the ceiling.

2) Measure the distance between the ceiling and the top of the baseboard. Add 6" to this measurement and cut off a length of the wallcovering.

3) Using the first strip as a guide, cut several lengths of the wallcovering and stack them face down on the long table.

4) Mix the powdered paste with water, following the instructions on the package.

5) Use the paste brush to apply paste to the back of the top strip, being extremely careful to coat all the edges thoroughly. Fold the strip twice, paste side in, so that the top and bottom edges meet at about the three-quarter mark. Put the strip aside for about 10 minutes so the paste can begin to set. In the meantime, you can paste and fold several more strips.

6) Take the first strip to the wall and open the top fold. Beginning at the ceiling, align the top third of the covering with the plumb line. In order to get the paper straight it may be necessary to overlap the ceiling molding, but it is essential that the edge of the covering follow the plumb line exactly. When the edge is in place, smooth it with the smoothing brush, working out from the center of the covering toward all the edges. Make certain there are no air bubbles anywhere.

When the top third of the covering is smooth and tight against the wall, peel open the bottom two thirds and smooth the entire strip in place along the plumb line, working from the center out. The covering will overlap the door or window; this overlap can be trimmed by running the trimming knife carefully down the crevice. The strip can also be trimmed at the top and along the baseboard. The essential point to remember about the first strip is that *it must be true with the plumb line.* If it is not, every successive strip will be crooked.

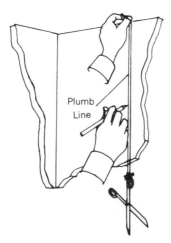

Plumb
Line

The most critical part of paper hanging is establishing a plumb line on each wall you are covering.

7) When the first strip is completely flat and shows no air bubbles anywhere, the second strip is applied to the wall by matching its design along the plumbed edge of the first strip.

To make the seam joint between the two strips, press the new strip against the wall lightly, with its edge about ¼″ away from the previous strip. Slide the strip into position, moving it up or down to align the pattern with that of the previous strip, and then smooth it against the wall in the same way you did the first strip. When the paste is partially dry (in about 10 or 15 minutes), use the seam roller to press the edges of the seam against the wall. Roll the cylinder of the roller up and down over the seam in short strokes until both strips have been completely flattened into place.

8) Continue applying strips along the wall toward the nearest room corner. Before the last strip is hung, measure the distance from the top and bottom of the corner to the edge of the covering. Add ½″ to the greater of the two measurements and cut the corner strip lengthwise. Hang the measured strip and trim it top and bottom.

9) Corners are notoriously crooked. As a result, each wall that is covered must begin with a plumbed strip. Establish the plumb line on the new wall ½″ closer to the corner than the width of the remaining part of the divided strip. Hang this cut strip along the plumb line, letting it overlap the corner. There will be a slight but unavoidable distortion of the pattern alignment at the corner. Most professionals, however, insist that the only area where patterns must be perfectly aligned is at eye level.

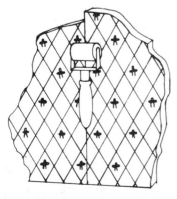

After two strips of wallcovering are in place, roller the seam to press the edges together.

10) When the walls have been covered with full-length strips, there will remain a number of tiny areas over doors, around windows and the like that can be covered with smaller, separate pieces. Cut the pieces so that their patterns match as nearly as possible with the adjacent strips and paste them in place.

Covering Ceilings

Installing wallcovering on ceilings is a difficult, tiring job and is best done with at least two people working. The ceiling must be thoroughly cleaned and smoothed, so the floor should be covered with a drop cloth or newspapers. While the actual procedure for applying a covering to ceilings is the same as for walls, there are some minor variations that should be observed.

1) To begin with, work across the narrow width of the room so that the strips will be shorter and more manageable. In order to reach the ceiling, place a stepladder at each side of the room and lay two 2"x10" planks nailed (or clamped) together across the steps, so that you have a simple scaffold to walk along.

2) Since a plumb line cannot be used, stretch a piece of string across the ceiling. Position it 1" closer to the parallel wall than the width of the wallcovering. Rub the string with colored chalk and tie it tautly onto two tacks driven into either end of the ceiling (or its molding). At a point about halfway between the tacks, pull the string down from the ceiling and let it snap back. It will leave a chalk line on the ceiling, which becomes your guideline for the first strip of covering.

3) Cut all the strips needed to cover the ceiling at one time. Each strip should be long enough to span the room, plus 4" for trim allowance.

4) After brushing paste on a strip, accordion-fold it. Do not let the patterned side touch any of the paste, and be sure not to crease the paper.

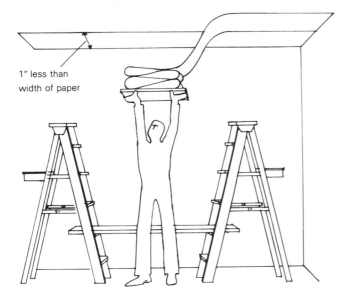

1" less than
width of paper

It is hard enough to paper a ceiling without inhibiting your movements as well, so set up a simple scaffold and, if possible, use a helper.

When attaching a strip to the ceiling, one person should be on the scaffold pressing the covering into place while the other holds the remainder of the strip, opening it fold by fold and checking the alignment of the pasted section as it is put in place.

5) After the strip is in place, follow the same procedures for smoothing and rollering wallcovering on a wall. Then use a clean paint roller attached to a mop handle to smooth the strip firmly against the ceiling and eliminate any bubbles that may have been missed.

Wallpaper Repairs

Wallpaper does not offer any problems except one — sometimes it develops bubbles. To eliminate a bubble, make an **X**-shaped cut in it with a razor, then pull back the resulting flaps and coat them with white or cream glue. Push the flaps tightly against the wall and use your seam roller to make them flat.

EIGHT

House Plumbing System

EVERY HOME PLUMBING SYSTEM IS COMPOSED OF three areas: the water supply system, the fixtures and the drain-waste-vent system. Fresh water is brought into the house under pressure and distributed to the various fixtures by the water supply pipes. The fixtures are all the outlets — sinks, toilets and tubs — where you use that fresh water. When you are finished with the water, it drains out of the house by way of the drain-waste-vent system.

WATER SUPPLY SYSTEM

Fresh water comes from a well or a municipal water system and enters your house under pressure. It immediately passes through a main shutoff valve which you can use to turn off all the water in the house anytime there is an emergency. The cold water main supplies water to your hot water heater and, at the same time, begins a parallel run of hot and cold water pipes that extend up through the walls of the building. The water supply pipes are usually ¾" pipe, although they may be as large as 1" or as small as ½" in diameter. Both cold and hot water mains go to each

Where you will find the plumbing systems in your house.

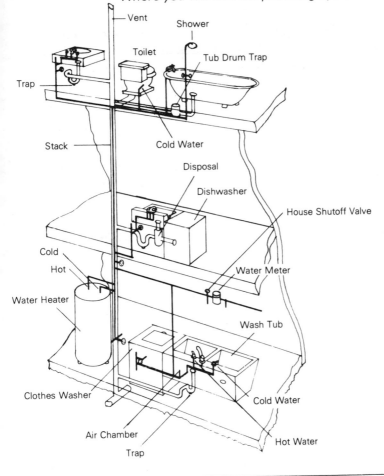

It is a good idea to tag all the water valves in your house so that if there is an emergency you can quickly find which ones to shut off.

fixture in the house (except toilets, which require only cold water), so they almost always are found next to each other.

Three-eighths-inch or ½" pipes lead from the hot and cold mains to each fixture. Traditionally, the cold water is connected to the right-hand faucet and the hot to the left. Attached to each supply pipe entering a fixture is a 1' capped pipe known as an *air chamber*. Air chambers are shock absorbers that fill with excess water, preventing pipe vibration and equalizing water pressure when a faucet is turned off abruptly and several hundred pounds of pressure develop in the supply mains.

Throughout the water supply system, you will find valves at various points. A good plumbing system has a shutoff valve wherever the hot and cold water mains emerge from the wall near a fixture, and still other valves placed along horizontal pipes and at the base of any pipe that runs vertically through the house. Having all these valves allows you to shut off the water supply to different parts of the plumbing system without affecting the plumbing in the rest of the house.

FIXTURES

The most visible parts of your home's plumbing system are the fixtures—the toilet, bathtub, sink, lavatory and shower. A fixture is designed to collect water in a receptacle that can be emptied anytime you wish, which means every fixture includes both a faucet and a drain. The water reaches a fixture via faucets; the drain, or receptacle part of the fixture, is connected to the drain-waste-vent system, which expels the water from the house after it has been used.

DRAIN-WASTE-VENT SYSTEM

Commonly referred to as the DWV, the drain-waste-vent system is made up of vents, traps, waste pipes and a soil stack, all of which carry water away from the fixtures.

When you drain a sink or bathtub, or flush a toilet, the used water flows into *waste pipes,* which are between 1½" and 2" in diameter and immediately attached to a curved piece of pipe known as a *trap.* Traps are designed to hold a small amount of water after a sink is drained or a bathtub emptied. The water prevents gases and vermin from migrating up the soil stack, through the waste pipes and out the fixtures into the house. Sinks and lavatories (the technical name for bathroom sinks) usually have either P- or S-shaped traps; toilets have built-in traps, in that the bowl is designed to retain water at all times.

The pipe attached to the trap is between 1¼" and 2" in diameter and is known as the *fixture waste pipe.* It is always sloped, so that waste water will flow away from the fixture, directly to the soil stack.

The *soil stack* is a 3" or 4" pipe that goes vertically from the building drain at the bottom of the house to the roof, where it is capped by an open vent. The stack has two purposes: to let air into the plumbing system, thus keeping the traps from being siphoned dry every time water rushes through them; and to allow

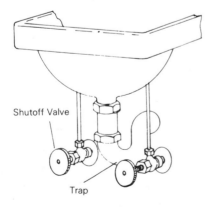

Shutoff Valve

Trap

The shutoff valves for fixtures are usually positioned where the pipes come out of the walls.

sewer gases to escape without putting pressure on the seals in the traps. A properly vented plumbing system keeps pressure in the pipes equalized so that waste and water can flow freely and no water will back up into any fixture stationed below a fixture that is draining. Every trap in the house is, or should be, vented directly to the stack; technically, the section of pipe in the stack immediately above a fixture is designated as a *vent*; the part below is the *waste line*.

All waste and used water eventually collects in the large horizontal pipe at the bottom of the house known as the *building drain*. This drain is pitched so that waste can flow down to the street sewer or house septic tank and is fitted with a *cleanout assembly* at the highest end of its run. The cleanout has a removable cover so you can open the pipe if it ever becomes clogged. Cleanout plugs usually are located at the base of the stack and anywhere the waste line changes direction. Some houses also have a large U-shaped trap situated just before the building drain exits the house; many fixture traps also have a cleanout plug.

PIPES AND TUBING

Fittings

There is a complete range of fittings available for each kind of pipe used in plumbing; it is safe to assume that no matter what you want to join, there is a fitting available to do the job. Fittings allow a pipe run to go around corners and branch off at different angles, and connect different sizes and even different kinds of pipe together. Some of the principal types are shown here. But in order to buy a fitting you must be able to give its proper size, and this is where plumbing gets to be a little confusing.

Pipes are referred to by the *nominal* diameter of their inside circumference. However, a ¾" pipe, which you might think is ¾" inside, is liable to be slightly more or less than that. Furthermore, its outside diameter will be closer to an inch. So when you are determining the size of a pipe, measure the *inside* diameter carefully and don't be surprised if the measurement is more or less than its stated ½", ¾" or 1" size.

If you buy a T or Y fitting, always state the *run-through size* first, then the *branch size*. For example, a T that will allow a ½" pipe to branch off a ¾" pipe run would be designated as a ¾"x¾"x½" T. The reason for the three dimensions is that some fittings can reduce the size of the pipe run. Whenever possible, take pieces of the pipe you are fitting to the store with you to make sure they fit in the fittings you are purchasing.

Galvanized Steel Pipe

Galvanized pipe is the most common pipe found in plumbing. It rarely leaks and can withstand high pressures. The major difficulty in working with galvanized steel pipe is that it must be threaded in order to make a joint. It also tends to corrode or form a scale from some kinds of water, so your local plumbing code may not allow you to use it.

Galvanized steel and brass fittings.

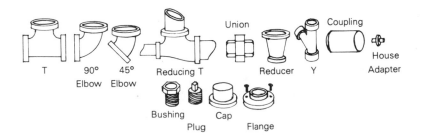

T   90° Elbow   45° Elbow   Reducing T   Union   Reducer   Y   Coupling   House Adapter

Bushing   Plug   Cap   Flange

Brass Pipe

Brass is more expensive than other pipe and must also be threaded, but it provides the best water supply system available. It is as strong as galvanized steel, can withstand pressure and is so smooth that water flowing through it meets with little resistance.

Copper Pipe and Tubing

Copper pipe is versatile and easy to install. It is available in various sizes from plumbing supply stores. It resists corrosion and can be used in both water supply and DWV systems. There are two kinds of copper pipe: *soft-tempered (tubing)*, which is flexible enough to bend around corners, and *hard-tempered,* which is rigid enough to be used in long runs.

Flexible tubing is used to connect the water supply mains with the fixtures. The tubing sizes used in your house system are nominally ⅜″, ½″ and ¾″, with their outside diameters measuring ⅛″ thicker. The inside diameters of copper pipe are usually pretty close to their nominal sizes, but the wall thickness of rigid copper pipe can vary considerably.

Copper fittings.

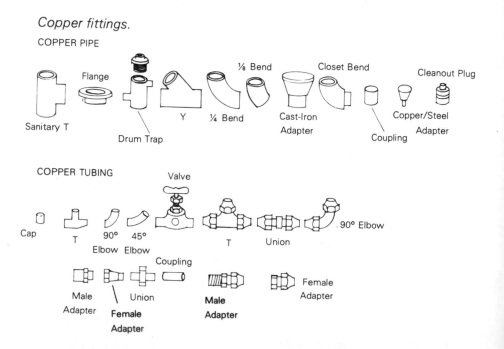

COPPER PIPE

Sanitary T   Flange   Drum Trap   Y   ¼ Bend   ⅛ Bend   Cast-Iron Adapter   Closet Bend   Coupling   Copper/Steel Adapter   Cleanout Plug

COPPER TUBING

Cap   T   90° Elbow   45° Elbow   Valve   T   Union   90° Elbow

Male Adapter   Female Adapter   Union   Coupling   Male Adapter   Female Adapter

Plastic Pipe and Tubing

There are several types of plastic pipe. Polyethylene (PE) is flexible and comes in coils. It is used most often to bring water up from a well or as an underground service from a well or water main to the house, since it is manufactured in thicknesses to withstand 80, 100, 125 or 160 pounds per square inch (psi).

Polyvinylchloride (PVC) pipe is rigid enough to be used for both water service and drainage systems.

Acrylonitrile-butadiene-styrene (ABS) is black and used in the DWV system. Although it is not recommended, you can interchange PVC and ABS pipe.

Chlorinated polyvinylchloride (CPVC) is one of the plastic pipes you can use for a water supply system because it is chemically strengthened to withstand pressures of up to 100 psi, and up to 180°F. You can buy it in either ¾" or ½" diameters, both of which come in rigid 10' lengths. The fittings for CPVC pipe are as extensive as those for galvanized steel or copper.

Polybutylene (PB) pipe can be used for both hot and cold water supply lines. You can get it in ½", ⅜" and ¾" diameters that are sold in either 10' rigid lengths or 100' flexible coils.

Polyethylene (PE) tubing is widely used for connecting sinks and toilets to the water supply. It is flexible and is sold in long coils that have inside diameters of ½", ¾", 1" and larger.

Plastic fittings.

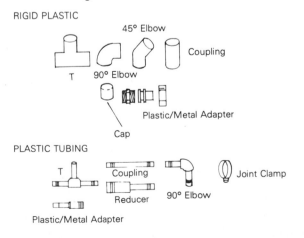

RIGID PLASTIC

45° Elbow
T   90° Elbow   Coupling
Cap   Plastic/Metal Adapter

PLASTIC TUBING

T   Coupling   90° Elbow   Joint Clamp
Reducer
Plastic/Metal Adapter

JOINING PLASTIC PIPE. Whether you are joining **PVC**, **ABS**, **CPVC**, **PB** or **PE**, the procedure is always the same. You can cut plastic pipe with a knife or your saber saw, but you must join it with a special solvent-welded adhesive. Your only problem is that once a joint is set, there is no way of changing it short of cutting the fitting out of the pipe and starting all over again. Follow this procedure:

1) When you measure plastic pipe, allow for the amount of pipe that goes into the fitting. Socket depths will vary, so measure them carefully and add the distances to the pipe length.

2) Cut the pipe with a fine-toothed saw blade and shave the burrs left on the inside of the pipe with a knife. Then sand the rough outside edges.

3) Test the pipe in its fitting. The joint should be tight enough so that the fitting does not slide off the pipe when you hold it upside down. Remove the fitting.

4) Wipe the pipe and the fitting clean with a cloth and apply solvent cement to both the inside of the fitting and the outside of the pipe. Be swift — in less than 60 seconds the cement will be dry. Place the fitting on the end of the pipe and twist it until it will go no further, then rotate it in the direction you want it to go and hold it in place for 10 seconds. If you have made the joint correctly, there will be a bead of dissolved plastic around the edge of the fitting. The joint will be set within 30 seconds, but don't try to move it for three minutes. It will be strong enough to take water pressure after an hour, but it is better to wait at least 16 hours before pressure-testing it.

Rigid plastic pipe can be joined to copper tubing with flare fittings, and to galvanized steel with a special coupling that is threaded on one end to fit into the steel pipe, and serrated on the other end. The serrated end squeezes into the plastic pipe and is secured with a worm-driven pipe clamp.

REPAIRS

The majority of repairs that you need to do in your plumbing system will be concentrated around the fixtures. Most of the plumbing system has no moving parts; the pipes are all connected in one way or another and there they sit, unmolested, for years. But the faucets have handles that turn, and the fixture drain traps are always busy collecting debris that is too large to move through the DWV. These are the places where trouble is most likely to appear and demand your attention.

Materials

As you wrestle with your plumbing system, you will usually have a wrench, a screwdriver or a pair of pliers in your hand; you will also need some washers and a roll of Teflon tape.

WASHERS. Buy a 59¢ box of assorted washers. They are little rubber disks with a small hole in the center which is exactly the size of the half-dozen brass screws that also come in the box. The washers are various diameters and at least one of the assortment is bound to fit any faucet or valve.

When you are replacing a washer, unscrew the existing disk and put a new washer in its place. You will notice as you tighten the retaining screw that it tends to flatten the raised center of the washer so that the washer can tightly seal the assembly.

TEFLON TAPE. Until recently, every plumbing connection had to have at least putty, and often putty and string, wrapped around the threads of the pipe to seal the union. Now everybody uses Teflon tape, which is a thin, white plastic that is wrapped tightly two or three times around the threads of the pipe. The tape is so thin that it settles into the grooves of the threads, sealing them against water leaking out of the joint. As a rule of thumb, always wrap Teflon tape around any pipe you are connecting. It can't hurt, and most often it will help.

WRENCHING EXPERIENCES. Wrenches are designed to give you leverage when you are tightening a pipe or its fitting. The pipe wrench, in particular, is so formidable that with very little effort you can crank a pipe so deeply into its fitting that you split the metal.

The threaded end of a pipe is cone-shaped, so the more threads you wind into a fitting, the tighter the joint becomes. Figure that if you can see four or five threads above a joint, the pipe is about as tight as you can safely get it. It is better to undertighten than to go too far. If the joint leaks, all you have to do is tighten it. If the fitting splits, you have to buy a new one and start all over again.

The escutcheons, or covers, and other shiny elements of faucets can be scratched and marred by the jaws of your wrenches. So before you lay wrench to chrome, first wrap the element with black electrician's tape. Not only will it protect the finish, but it will give the wrench a better grip.

Faucets

While faucets vary widely in design and appearance, all of them are repaired in much the same manner.

REPAIRING A STANDARD FAUCET. Follow this procedure:

1) Turn off both the hot and the cold water valves nearest the fixture.

2) Open the faucet handle and let all the water in the fixture drain off.

3) Some faucets have caps marked "Hot" and "Cold" which hide the handle screws. Pry the caps loose with the blade of your screwdriver and remove the screw in the top of the handle.

4) Lift the faucet handle from the stem shank by pulling it straight up. If the handle resists you, tap it gently and evenly around the bottom with the handle of a screwdriver, or use the blade as a pry to push the handle upward. *Do not force the handle*. It could break, or the stem knurling could be damaged.

5) Inspect the handle carefully. If the handle or its threads appear damaged, replace the handle.

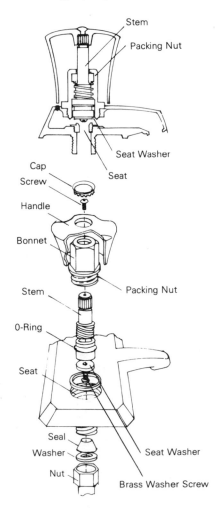

Anatomy of a standard faucet.

6) Wrap friction tape around the faucet bonnet to protect the metal finish, then loosen the bonnet with your adjustable wrench.

7) Inspect the bonnet packing or stem washer (it will have one or the other). If the packing is compressed or worn or if the washer is chewed up, replace.

8) The faucet stem is now fully visible; remove it from the faucet body by hand-turning it.

9) Inspect the knurling at the stem top, as well as the threads on the stem body. If either is worn, the stem must be replaced.

10) The seat washer is held to the base of the stem assembly by a brass screw. Unthread the screw and inspect the washer for wear, compression or damage. If the washer is in any way less than perfect, replace it.

11) Once you have removed the faucet stem, you can inspect the faucet seat for any damage. If the seat is an integral part of the faucet and is severely damaged, the entire faucet assembly has to be replaced. If the seat is removable, unscrew it from the faucet body and replace it.

12) After you have inspected the entire unit, begin reassembling the unit by hand-turning the stem in the faucet body, then tightening it with a wrench. The faucet stem should not be in the fully closed position. Keep it open so that the stem washer does not bind in the faucet body.

13) Place the stem washer over the stem shank, and make sure the washer is seated squarely.

14) Put the bonnet packing back on, or place the packing washer over the stem washer.

15) Place the bonnet over the stem shank and tighten by hand. Finish tightening the bonnet with a wrench until it is snug. Do not overtighten, or you will either strip the threads or compress the packing.

16) Place the handle on the stem and replace the handle screw.

17) Turn the handle to the fully closed position and snap the faucet caps in place.

18) Open the water valves and turn the handles on and off to test for leakage. If there is any leakage, tighten the bonnet another quarter turn.

19) Remove the friction tape from the bonnet.

WASHERLESS FAUCETS. Some washerless faucets may have an insert in the center of the knob that must be pried up to expose the handle screw. Once the handle is removed, you usually will not find any packing nut or packing washer, but there is a stem nut that must be rotated counterclockwise with a wrench before you can lift the assembly out of the faucet body.

Washerless faucets sometimes have O-ring seals around the outside of their bodies which may resist being removed. Put the handle back on the stem so that you can grip the assembly without using pliers or a wrench, which might damage the metal. Using the handle you can now pull the valve assembly from the body.

Washerless faucets often have a rubber diaphragm or rotating disks at their base to control the water flow. Because there are no washers, these faucets rarely develop any problems except for an occasional worn metal part.

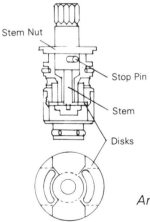

Stem Nut

Stop Pin

Stem

Disks

Anatomy of a washerless faucet.

TUB FAUCETS. In many cases the water supply valves that control the lines servicing a bathtub are as far away as the basement. When there is an access panel to the piping in the wall behind the fixtures, the shutoff valve will be found near the tub.

Bathtub faucets normally are set in the wall above the drain end of the tub. Most of them have a large escutcheon that has to be removed before you can repair the faucet. In some instances you will need a pair of vise-grip pliers with wide-opening jaws to remove the escutcheon, but it can often be pried off with a screwdriver blade. Once the escutcheon is removed, you can take the faucet apart by following the same procedures used for disassembling a standard faucet (see page 122).

MIXER FAUCETS. Mixer faucets combine hot and cold water before the water comes out of a single spigot. When a mixer faucet develops a leak, the entire internal cartridge has to be replaced. The handle may have a threaded cap over the screw. Remove the cap, handle and escutcheon, then pull the stop tube off the body and pry the retainer clip out of the front of the body. Now pull the cartridge from the body and insert a new cartridge, preferably one from the same manufacturer. As you slide the new cartridge in place, push it into the faucet body until the front edges of its ears are flush with the lip of the body. The retainer clip legs must straddle the cartridge and lock in the bottom slot of the body.

Anatomy of a tub or shower mixer faucet.

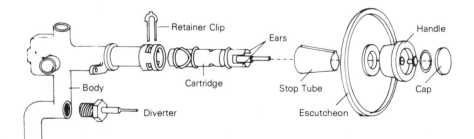

SINK SPRAY HOSES. When a sink spray hose stops working, first unscrew the aerators in both the faucet and the spray head and check them for clogging. If the aerators are damaged or cannot be cleaned, replace them.

Next, examine the hose to see if it is kinked. Should the hose appear to be clogged or damaged in any way, undo the hex nut connector at the base of the faucet, and either repair or replace the hose. If the hose still doesn't work, remove the faucet spout by unscrewing the O-ring at its base to expose the diverter valve assembly. The diverter valve can be either pulled or unscrewed from the faucet base and then disassembled for cleaning and inspection. If any of its parts are worn, the entire valve should be replaced.

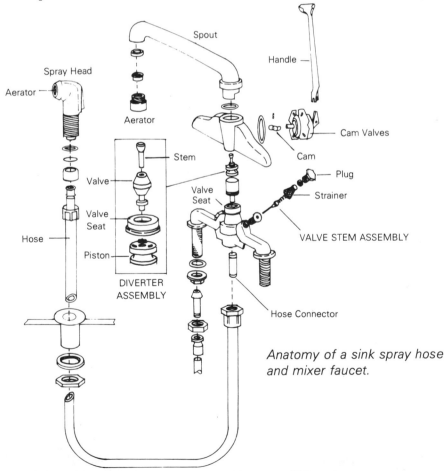

Anatomy of a sink spray hose and mixer faucet.

DISK VALVE FAUCETS. The two long screws located on either side of the handle stem hold the entire unit together. Once you unscrew them, the top half of the base can be pulled off. Also remove the movable top disk which rotates with the handle stem to open and close holes in the fixed disk at the bottom of the faucet body. While none of the metal parts in the disk valve faucet will wear out, the inlet seals can deteriorate and need to be replaced.

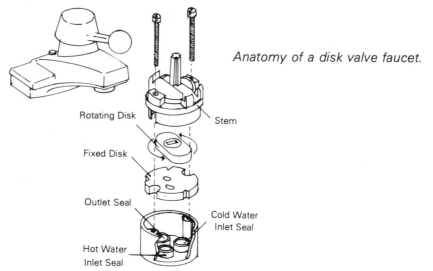

Anatomy of a disk valve faucet.

Rotating Disk

Stem

Fixed Disk

Outlet Seal

Cold Water Inlet Seal

Hot Water Inlet Seal

FAUCET TROUBLESHOOTING CHART

Problem: Drips at spout

POSSIBLE CAUSE	REMEDY
Faucet partially open	Turn faucet handle until tightly closed.
Handle or stem defective	**If threads on stem or handle are worn, replace part.**

Seat washer worn	Remove the handle and stem. Examine the seat washer on the bottom of the stem and replace it if it is worn or chewed.
Seat worn	Remove the handle and stem. Examine the faucet seat in the bottom of the faucet body for wear or roughness. You can buy a seat dresser which will regrind the seat, making it smooth. But many faucets have threaded seats which can be replaced by unscrewing them and inserting a new seat. If the seat is a part of the faucet body, you will have to replace the entire faucet.

Problem: Spout drips; faucet noisy, vibrates

POSSIBLE CAUSE	REMEDY
Stem defective; seat washer loose	Remove the faucet stem and examine it closely for any defects. If the threads are worn or the metal pitted, buy an identical replacement at a plumbing supply store. If the seat washer is loose, tighten the brass screw that holds it. If the noise and/or vibration persists, the entire faucet should be replaced.

Problem: Handle turns but water still runs

POSSIBLE CAUSE	REMEDY
Handle or stem defective	Remove the handle. Examine the threads on the handle and stem. If either is worn, replace the appropriate part.

Problem: Water leaks at handle

POSSIBLE CAUSE	REMEDY
Bonnet packing or washer faulty	Remove the handle, bonnet and packing nut. Examine the packing nut for compressed or crumbling packing. If defective, replace with new packing. If the faucet has a bonnet washer and it is worn or chewed, replace it.

Problem: Mixer faucet leaks at swivel

POSSIBLE CAUSE	REMEDY
Spout bonnet loose	Tighten the bonnet with a wrench.
Spout packing or washer defective	Remove the spout and spout bonnet. Inspect the bonnet packing or washer and replace if defective.

Problem: Mixer faucet leaks at base

POSSIBLE CAUSE	REMEDY
Mixing chamber faulty	Replace the faucet. Mixing chambers are almost impossible to repair successfully.

Problem: Reduced water flow from spout

POSSIBLE CAUSE	REMEDY
Aerator screen clogged	Unscrew the aerator nozzle at the end of the spout. Clean the aerator screen thoroughly or replace it if it is broken.
Nozzle defective	If the screen and washers attached to the nozzle are badly worn or heavily coated with mineral deposits, replace it.

Toilets

A toilet consists of a vitreous china bowl placed on the floor and connected to the DWV by a waste pipe at its base. The top of the bowl usually has a plastic molded seat and cover. Above and behind the bowl is a vitreous china water tank which is placed over a water-inlet port at the back of the bowl. The bowl has a second hole in its bottom or side for the cold water supply, which is attached to a flush valve that automatically controls the water entering and leaving the unit.

When the flush valve develops problems it is possible to buy replacement parts. But a complete new flush valve costs only about $7, so it is more practical to put in a new one. If you do replace the flush valve assembly, purchase one of the new Fluid Level Control (FLC) valves. The FLC has fewer parts that can break and eliminates the need for a float ball. It also has a very definite action that shuts off the water and is virtually noise free.

Water runs; tank does not fill	Examine the handle, trip lever, flapper, lift rods or chain, and the float ball to be sure they are not binding against anything. If any of them bind or get stuck, bend the part in whatever direction will allow it to work properly.

Tank fills but water still runs (hissing sound)

Lift the float ball. If the hissing stops, bend the float arm slightly downward. If that fails, undo the two setscrews holding the valve assembly and pull the inlet valve out of its seat. Clean the valve seat if it is corroded and replace the small seat washer at the bottom of the valve if it is worn. Check the flapper to be sure it is seated properly.

Water level too high or too low

The water should be ¾" below the top of the overflow pipe. You can bend the float arm up to raise the water level, or down to lower it. The FLC unit has a clip on a traveller rod that lets you raise or lower the float unit.

Partial flush

The flapper is not opening enough. Bend the upper lift rod or shorten the lift chain.

INSTALLING A TOILET FLUSH VALVE.   Follow this procedure:

1) Shut off the water supply valve. Flush the toilet to empty the tank and sponge out the remaining water.

2) Using a pipe wrench, loosen the nut under the tank that connects the tail pipe of the flush valve to the water supply pipe.

3) Unscrew the locknut that is flush against the bottom of the tank and lift the valve and float ball assemblies out of the tank. There may be a rubber refill tube clipped to the top of the overflow pipe. Just pull it off the pipe.

4) The new unit comes with a rubber washer that slides over the valve tail pipe and fits flush against the bottom of the valve. With the washer in place, stand the replacement valve in its hole in the tank and hand-tighten the locknut on the tail pipe protruding through the bottom of the tank. Finish tightening it with approximately one half-turn of your pipe wrench.

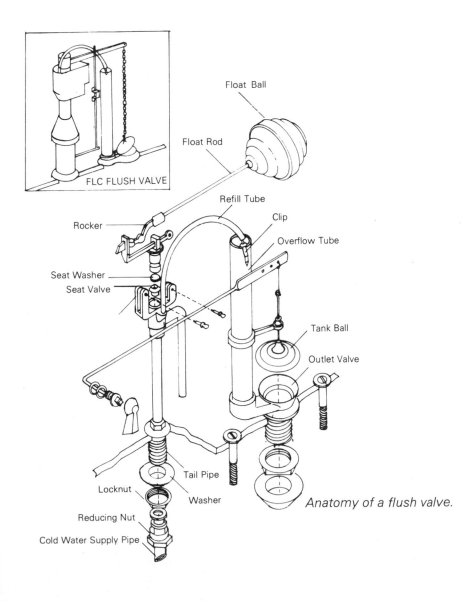

FLC FLUSH VALVE

Float Ball

Float Rod

Refill Tube

Rocker

Clip

Overflow Tube

Seat Washer

Seat Valve

Tank Ball

Outlet Valve

Tail Pipe

Locknut

Washer

Reducing Nut

Cold Water Supply Pipe

Anatomy of a flush valve.

5) The tubing that leads from the water supply valve may have a flanged end, or it may be straight. Most replacement valves come with the washers and nuts needed to attach either type of tubing to the valve tail pipe, as well as instructions for assembly. The washer is placed over the end of the tube, and the small tubing is united to the tail pipe with a large reducing nut. Tighten the nut one half-turn with your wrench.

6) If the new unit is an FLC valve, it is ready to work as soon as the refill tube is attached to the nipple on the top of the valve assembly and clipped to the top of the overflow tube, because it does not have a float ball. If the new assembly is a float valve, unscrew the float ball and float rod from the old assembly and attach them to the new one.

7) Replace the tank top and turn on the water supply valve. Observe all connections as the tank is filling to be sure they are not leaking. If any of them leak, tighten them only until the drip stops.

TOILET TROUBLESHOOTING CHART

Problem: Water continues running

POSSIBLE CAUSE	REMEDY
Tank stopper does not seat or is faulty	Flush the toilet and watch the action of the stopper ball or flapper. If the stopper is connected to the lift lever by rods, you can bend the upper rod to realign the stopper ball. If the flapper is connected to a chain, be sure it is long enough to allow the flapper to close and short enough so that it does not get caught under the flapper when it raises. If the ball or flapper is damaged in any way, replace it.

Float ball faulty	Unscrew the ball from the float rod and inspect it for cracks or punctures. If water can enter the ball, replace it.
Inlet valve faulty	Remove the setscrews holding the inlet valve to the flush valve assembly. If the seat washer is worn, replace it. If the inlet valve is defective, replace the entire flush valve.
Overflow tube defective	Unscrew the overflow tube and examine it for corrosion or leaks. If damaged, replace it.

Problem: Tank does not flush

POSSIBLE CAUSE	REMEDY
Lift lever assembly faulty	Flush the toilet. Observe the action of the handle, lift rod, and guide rods or chain. They should not bind; bend any binding parts so that they can move smoothly. If the handle is defective, replace it.
Inlet valve faulty	Remove the inlet valve and examine it for worn or defective parts. Either replace the faulty parts or replace the entire flush valve.

Problem: Toilet tank leaks

POSSIBLE CAUSE	REMEDY
Tank damaged	Inspect the sides and bottom of the tank for cracks or deep chips. If the tank is damaged it must be replaced. Undo the

bolts in the bottom of the tank and unscrew the outlet leading to the bowl. Disconnect the water supply line attached to the flush valve tail pipe. Lift the tank off the toilet and replace with a similar tank.

Inlet supply valve faulty

Check the underside of the tank around the water supply line connections for leakage. Tighten any connections that drip water. Replace split or damaged pipes.

Outlet washer faulty or spud washer worn

Examine the area between the tank and bowl for leakage. If water appears when the toilet is flushed, disconnect the tank from the bowl and replace the washer.

Problem: Toilet leaks around its base

POSSIBLE CAUSE	REMEDY
Bowl damaged	Examine the bowl for cracks or large chips. If damaged, the bowl must be replaced.
Bowl loose	Rock the bowl. If it is loose, pry off the caps at the base of the bowl and tighten the nuts underneath them.
Ferrule loose; grout at base of bowl faulty	If there is leakage at the base of the bowl, it must be removed and the ferrule and lead bend inspected. If work must be done on the lead drainage bend, it is suggested that you hire a professional.

Unclogging drains

The most common repairs that must be done on sinks and lavatories involve clogged drains. The first thing to do is reach into the water and clear away any debris that may have collected over the drain. The next step is to use a rubber force cup, also known as a plumber's friend or plunger.

A force cup, if used properly, can solve a lot of problems, and the best kind to buy is one with a fold-down rim so that it can be used on both sinks and toilets. The force cup, by the way, works best when there are several inches of hot water in the basin to act as a seal for the cup and also to help melt whatever grease may be in the drain.

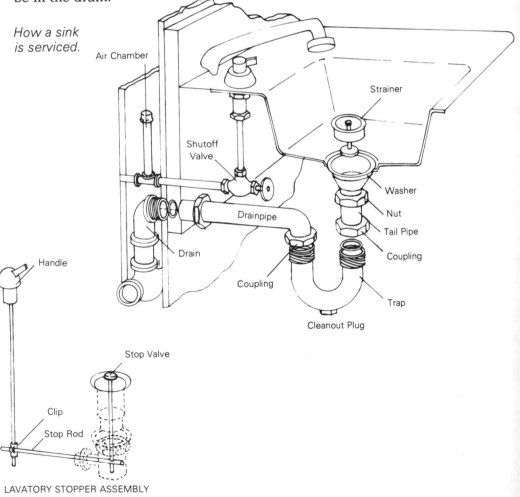

How a sink is serviced.

Air Chamber

Strainer

Shutoff Valve

Washer

Drainpipe

Nut

Tail Pipe

Drain

Coupling

Handle

Coupling

Trap

Cleanout Plug

Stop Valve

Clip

Stop Rod

LAVATORY STOPPER ASSEMBLY

USING A FORCE CUP.   Follow this procedure:

1) Remove the stopper in the sink or lavatory. Lavatories and bathtubs have overflow openings which must be plugged with a damp cloth so that the pressure from the force cup does not escape through the overflow.

2) Tilt the force cup to one side to fill it with water, then place it squarely over the drain.

3) Push the handle down and then up, five or six times. On the final upward stroke, yank the cup sharply off the drain. This may cause a geyser of water, but it will also exert tremendous pressure on the clog.

OTHER UNCLOGGING OPTIONS.   When the force cup doesn't clear a blockage, you have three options, two of which are dangerous. Your first option is an auger. You can make a serviceable auger just by straightening out a coat hanger. Or you can purchase a drain auger at any plumbing supply or hardware store. The *stranded drain auger,* or *snake,* is a tough, flexible cable or tape that can be pushed into the cleanout plug at the bottom of a sink trap, through the waste pipe and all the way to the stack. The tape augers cannot be rotated, but must be pounded against the clog; the cable snakes have a handle that you turn, so you are actually drilling the cable into the clog. The closet auger, made only for toilets, has a sharp bend so that it can reach up into the toilet trap as far as the outlet horn, where most clogging occurs.

Your second option is the *compressed air cleaner.* This fires a bolt of compressed air down the drain which should blast the blockage free. Air tools work pretty well but they have been known to blow apart old pipes in the process. Unless your plumbing is brand new, don't risk using a compressed air tool.

Your third choice is to use a *chemical drain opener.* There are dozens of these on the market and very few professional plumbers will go near them because they are not only harmful to humans, but they can eat holes in your drainpipes as well. If you *must* use one of them, at least be meticulous about following the instructions on the package.

In order to clean the trap in almost any drain, use your pipe wrench to unscrew the metal plug near the bottom of the curve in the trap, or loosen the couplings on both ends of the curved pipe. Remember to place a pan under the pipe before you remove the plug—the trap is supposed to hold water, as well as catch anything too large to go down the drain. Once the cap or the entire trap is removed you can begin probing the drain with whatever auger you are using.

Cleanout Plug   Trap

The trap plug is found at the lowest point in the curve of the drain.

TUB DRAINS. Many bathtubs are equipped with a drum-shaped trap located in the floor under an access panel. The clean-out plug in the top of this drum must be unscrewed.

If you can't find the access panel, the tub's drainage system is probably reached either from the floor below or through a panel in the wall behind the tub. When you locate it you will most likely encounter a P- or S-shaped trap similar to the ones on your sinks and lavatories.

The blockage that occurs in tubs is often at the stopper mechanism rather than the trap, so when your tub is clogged, check the stopper first. Some stoppers have a spring that puts pressure against the rod assembly. This in turn raises and lowers the stopper when the lever is flipped. The spring can accumulate a lot of lint, hair and other debris that will eventually cause a blockage in the drain. To reach the spring, unscrew the escutcheon plate over the stopper lever, grip the drain trip-lever handle, and pull the entire mechanism up and out of the tub. Thoroughly clean the assembly before replacing it.

Tubs with a weight-type stopper often will accumulate dirt on the bottom of the weight so that it cannot fit snugly into its seat. As a result, water trickles out of the tub even when you close the drain. Unscrew the escutcheon and pull out the stopper lever and its weight. Thoroughly clean the entire unit, paying particular attention to the bottom of the weight. Before reinstalling the stopper assembly, run hot water in the tub for several minutes to wash away any dirt clinging to the stopper seat.

If the lever on a stopper mechanism does not stay in position when it is depressed, remove the mechanism and examine it for a worn or broken spring, or other worn parts; these should be replaced.

Emergency Repairs

No matter what causes a plumbing problem, your first reaction should be to shut off the nearest water valves. If it is easier and quicker, close the main water supply valve, located somewhere near the water meter or at the point where the main service enters the house. With no more water flowing through your plumbing system, you now have plenty of time to find the source of trouble and perform at least emergency repairs, if not solve the problem once and for all.

If a pipe splits, sooner or later you will have to replace the entire damaged section. For immediate repair, provided the damage is no more than 4″ in length, there are two solutions: a dresser coupling or a compression clamp.

USING A DRESSER COUPLING. Follow this procedure:

1) Close the valve controlling the flow of water through the pipe.

2) Turn on the nearest fixtures to drain as much water as possible from the pipe.

3) Cut the pipe approximately 1″ beyond either side of the damaged area, but do not remove more than a 6″ length of pipe.

4) Unscrew the compression collars at each end of the dresser coupling body.

5) Place one collar on each end of the severed pipe.

6) Insert the main body of the coupling over the cut pipe ends and slide the collars over the ends of the coupling body.

7) Tighten the couplings by hand. Then complete the tightening, using two wrenches.

8) When the collars are tightened, turn on the water valve and inspect the connection for leaks. If any water appears, tighten the couplings until the leakage stops.

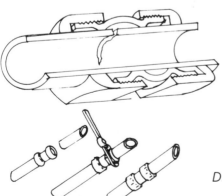

Dresser coupling and how to use it.

APPLYING A COMPRESSION CLAMP. The compression clamp is comprised of two curved pieces of metal lined with rubber or neoprene. The two halves are hinged together along one edge and have threaded screw or bolt holes on the opposite edge. The clamp must be large enough to fit around the pipe being repaired, and should extend at least 1″ beyond each side of the damaged area.

1) Shut off the valve controlling the water that flows through the damaged pipe.

2) Turn on the nearest fixture to drain off as much water as possible from the pipe.

3) Place the clamp around the damaged part of the pipe.

4) Insert bolts or screws in the threaded holes at the edge of the clamp and tighten, drawing the two halves together.

5) Open the water valve and allow water to flow through the pipe. If there is leakage at the clamp, tighten the clamp screws slowly until the leak stops.

If damage to a drainpipe is no more than a pinhole or short hairline crack, it can often be repaired by applying beeswax, or putty and tape. However, beeswax cannot be used on any hot or cold water supply line, where the water is pressurized. Use it only on drains.

A pipe clamp is tightened around the pipe with screws or bolts. You must use a clamp that is the proper size for the pipe you are mending.

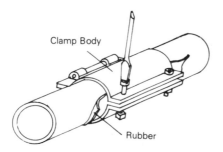

Clamp Body

Rubber

APPLYING BEESWAX. Follow this procedure:

1) Melt one end of a beeswax block until it reaches the consistency of putty. You can do this by putting the wax in a pan over a stove burner.

2) Force the beeswax into the pinhole or hairline crack until it builds up over the damage.

3) When the wax has cooled and hardened, wrap it with several layers of friction tape.

APPLYING PUTTY AND FRICTION TAPE. Follow this procedure:

1) Force commercial putty into the damaged area, completely filling the crack or hole and leaving a small mound of putty over the area.

2) Thoroughly clean the pipe adjacent to and around the putty so that the tape will stick to it properly.

3) Starting about 1″ away from the damaged area, wrap friction tape over the putty, stopping about 1″ beyond the damaged area.

4) Cut the tape and give the pipe a second wrapping in the opposite direction as the first layer.

REPAIRING FROZEN PIPES. Pipes that have frozen are in imminent danger of splitting, so treat them with care and patience. If an electric heating cable is available, you can wrap it around a frozen pipe, turn it on, then let it do its job. The pipe can also be wrapped in insulation, in which case it eventually will warm up enough for the water in it to begin flowing again.

If you feel called upon to do a lot of wet, hard work, you can dip some rags in hot water, wring them out and wrap them around the pipe. Naturally, the rags will cool off quickly, so you will have to change them every few minutes, but eventually they will melt the ice inside the pipe.

NINE

Home Electrical Work

ELECTRICITY IN YOUR HOME ORIGINATES IN A metal distribution box fastened to a wall in the cellar of your house or some other out-of-the-way place. The box is fed by a cable from your local power company. Just before the electricity reaches the box, a kilowatt-hour meter near it registers the amount of power you are using. If there is another box next to the meter, it contains a main circuit breaker or main switch that shuts off all the current entering the house. Otherwise, you will find the main switches marked "main" at the top of the distribution box itself.

Once the current enters the distribution box, it is divided into several branch circuits that extend through the house, each of which is protected by either a fuse or a circuit breaker as it carries electricity to the receptacles and switches attached to it.

When an electric appliance is plugged into an outlet and turned on, electricity immediately flows through one prong in the appliance's line plug and travels up one wire in the line cord, goes through the appliance and down the second wire in the cord, and returns to the branch circuit via the second prong on the appliance plug. Once back in the branch circuit cable, the current continues through the house and eventually returns to the distribution box, then back out of the house to the power company's electrical circuit.

DISTRIBUTION BOX

The distribution box is connected via the meter to the utility company's *feeder cable*. The feeder cable provides incoming service of 60, 100, 150 or 200 amps, which in turn is divided into the several *branch circuits* of 15, 20, 30 or more amps that make up the circuitry in the house. All of the cables in the branch circuits come together inside the distribution box. The *hot lines* (black or red) in each cable terminate at *fuses* or *circuit breakers,* which are designed to open a connection and stop current from flowing into that circuit. This stoppage of current flow will happen automatically if too much electricity enters the circuit. The *grounding wires* (white) in each cable are connected to a *bus bar* at the bottom of the box. This in turn is connected to a copper *grounding cable* or rod that is clamped to the nearest water pipe.

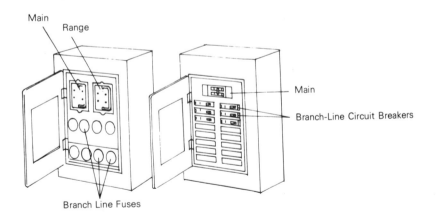

House fuse and circuit-breaker boxes look nearly alike and have the same function.

GROUNDING

Grounding plays so important a role in the home that many appliances come with their own green grounding wire attached to their line cords. Since electricity can follow any path, current leakage or a short circuit will travel directly to the highly conductive copper grounding cable and then into the earth via the water pipe.

If you touch an ungrounded appliance at the moment an electrical leakage occurs, and you also happen to be in contact with a radiator, sink or any metal unit that *is* connected to the ground, you will immediately become a path for the current to follow. But if the appliance is properly grounded via its green wire, it is connected to the house grounding system and the leakage current will travel back to the water pipe ground. An unusually large current flow or a short circuit results anytime two bare electrical wires come in contact. This will produce a surge of electricity, and the circuit breaker will immediately open or the fuse will blow, preventing any more current entering the branch circuit. Short circuits occur more often in appliances than in the house electrical system.

FUSES

There are four basic fuses used in house circuits: plug fuses, time-delay fuses, nontamperable fuses and cartridge fuses. All four types contain a short band of metal alloy with a low melting point. The size of this metal band determines the amount of current that the fuse can carry indefinitely. The instant a larger current passes through the band, the metal will melt, or "blow," and break the circle that the wires form, thereby opening the circuit. When one of these fuses blows, you can replace it by rotating it counterclockwise and removing it from its socket, then inserting a new fuse with the same rating (15, 20, 25 or 30 amps) printed on its face. Screw the new fuse into the socket so that current can once again flow through the line. If the new fuse also blows, begin looking for the source of trouble by consulting your wiring list (see page 151).

Fuses and circuit breakers found in the home.

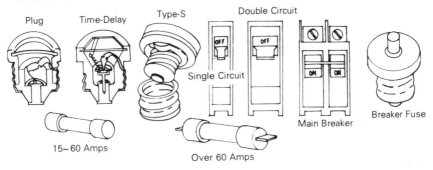

Plug Fuses

These are the most common of all fuses. You will find them attached to any circuit that feeds lightweight appliances. The metal band is positioned in a cylindrical housing with a threaded base and a glass window on the face of the unit. Plug fuses rated for 15, 20, 25 and 30 amps have round faces, while those rated for less than 15 amps are hexagonal in shape. When a plug fuse blows because of an overload, its window remains clear; if the cause is a short circuit, the window becomes blackened.

Time-Delay Fuses

Externally, a time-delay (or "slow-blow") fuse looks exactly like a plug fuse. But its metal band is soldered to a stretched spring anchored to the top of the unit just beneath the glass window. If a time-delay fuse blows because of a short circuit, its window will blacken the way any plug fuse does. If the time-delay fuse blows because of an overload, the solder at the bottom of the fuse softens, allowing the stretched spring to coil and break the circuit.

Time-delay fuses are useful in circuits that service such equipment as stationary power tools, air conditioners and washing machines, all of which require an extra surge of power when they are first turned on — this might blow a plug fuse.

Type-S Nontamperable Fuses

One drawback to fuses is that they can be misused. When a fuse on a given circuit begins blowing with any regularity, many people replace it with a higher-amperage fuse instead of reducing the load on the circuit. The higher-rated fuse allows more current into the circuit than the wires can handle, which may eventually cause a fire. Type-S nontamperable fuses were developed to prevent people from overfusing. They look like regular fuses and are sold in all the standard amperage ratings, but their bases are slightly smaller than regular fuses and the diameter of their bodies varies according to their amperage rating. The nontamps have reducing adapters that fit permanently in the fuse socket and cannot be removed without breaking the socket. The 15-amp adapter will accommodate only the 15-amp nontamp fuse. The 20-, 25- and 30-amp adapters will accept only a fuse with the matching rating.

Anytime you install a type-S fuse, be sure it is screwed in as tightly as possible. There is a spring in the bottom of the fuse that must make full contact with the adapter before the circuit will close.

Cartridge Fuses

These are used for the high-voltage lines needed to handle larger appliances such as ovens and house water heaters. They are sealed tubes that fit into clips. To change one, pull it out of its clips and insert a new fuse in its place.

CIRCUIT BREAKERS

Circuit breakers are made up of a manual switch and a bi-metal strip; outwardly, a circuit breaker looks like the some toggle switch used to control your light fixtures. The heat from current flowing through the bimetal strip causes the strip to bend. As long as the heat does not exceed the rating of the circuit, the switch remains in place. But an overload will cause the bimetal to become warped enough to break its contact and open the switch.

The breakers used for 120-volt circuits have separate off-on handles. For a 240-volt line, two breakers are joined at their handles so that no matter which half of the circuit has the overload, both sides snap open together. When a breaker opens, its handle jumps toward the "off" position. To reset it, you must push the handle beyond the "off" position, then move it back to "on."

Where the electrical wires go in your home.

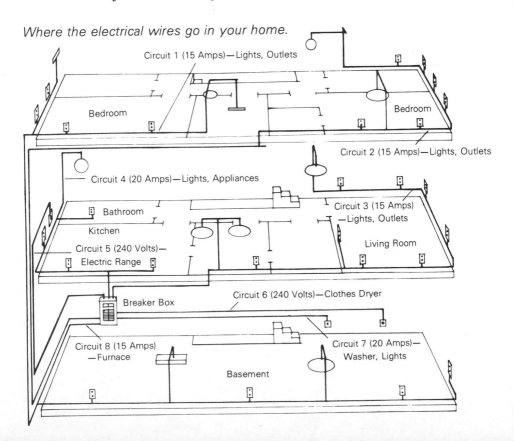

Circuit 1 (15 Amps)—Lights, Outlets

Bedroom

Bedroom

Circuit 2 (15 Amps)—Lights, Outlets

Circuit 4 (20 Amps)—Lights, Appliances

Circuit 3 (15 Amps) —Lights, Outlets

Bathroom

Kitchen

Living Room

Circuit 5 (240 Volts)— Electric Range

Breaker Box

Circuit 6 (240 Volts)—Clothes Dryer

Circuit 8 (15 Amps) —Furnace

Circuit 7 (20 Amps)— Washer, Lights

Basement

HOUSE CIRCUITS

There are two major kinds of circuits in your home: general purpose circuits and special appliance circuits. No matter how they are constructed or where they run, the number and type of outlets in your home, together with the total amount of power they will draw, have a great deal to do with how many separate circuits run through the house.

General Purpose Circuits

These circuits normally use #12 wire and provide a maximum of 20 amps. As a general rule, for every 400 square feet of floor area you should have one general purpose circuit for lamps, small appliances and light fixtures. Wiring in older houses may have used #14 wire with a maximum rating of 15 amps.

Special Appliance Circuits

These are needed for large appliances such as dishwashers, ranges, oil burners, water pumps and heaters, air conditioners, electric heaters, clothes dryers and workshop equipment. Each must have its own circuit rated at either 120 or 240 volts. Depending on the wattage requirements of the appliance, the circuit can be fused at 15, 20, 25 or 30 amps, but for the purposes of safety, the major appliance is often wired directly into the house circuit instead of using a plug and receptacle. There can also be a few outlets attached to the circuit, but never so many that the circuit is in danger of being overloaded. A pair of medium-size air conditioners, for example, might share the same circuit.

ELECTRICAL NEEDS AND CAPACITY

With the proliferation of ever more-powerful appliances requiring large amounts of electricity, almost every home eventually needs its electrical capacity upgraded. As a matter of both safety and convenience it is important for you to know whether each of the branch circuits in your home can handle all the appliances plugged into it. So before you do any upgrading, it is helpful to know exactly what the electrical capacity of the house is.

Wiring Check

There is a simple way of determining where each circuit in your house runs, and which appliances and lights each of them serves. Turn on all the lights in the house. Now remove any one of the branch-line fuses (or trip its breaker to the "off" position) and go through the house making up a list of which lights have gone out. Plug a small lamp or a test light into each outlet and be

WIRING CHECK FORM

Circuit #___	Outlet Location	Light Location	Appliance	Wattage
___ volts ×				
___ amps =				
___ watts				

Total Watts _____

sure to check such out-of-the-way places as closets, the garage and the attic. When one circuit has been completely checked and the whereabouts of each outlet listed, replace the fuse or reset the branch circuit breaker; then shut off another circuit. Continue logging the circuits one at a time until you have accounted for every light and outlet in the house.

Your completed wiring list should note which circuits serve each appliance and light. Now write down the wattage rating beside each appliance or light. The wattage is printed on the end of every light bulb; if it is not stamped on a particular appliance, use the average wattage given in the list shown here. Next, add up all the wattages on each circuit. The number you arrive at is the amount of wattage all the lights and appliances served by the circuit will need if all of them are drawing power at the same time.

Now multiply the amperage of the circuit (shown on the handle of its circuit breaker or the face of its fuse) times the house voltage (120-volt, 208-volt, 220-volt or 240-volt) to get the total power (wattage) of each circuit. The number you get is the amount of wattage each circuit is able to deliver without blowing a fuse. Compare the two wattages for each circuit to be sure none of the lines is being asked to deliver more power than it is capable of doing. A 120-volt circuit is at its capacity when the power use approaches 1800 watts on a 15-amp line, 2400 watts on a 20-amp line and 3600 watts on a 30-amp line. The total load on any circuit should not be more than 80% of its capacity if there are any motor-operated appliances on the line, since motors require an extra surge of electricity to start up.

INTERPRETING THE WIRING LIST. Most distribution boxes have space on the inside of their doors for you to list the location of each circuit that comes into the box. This is a good place to put the wiring list for future reference; the list tells you what appliances are in the house at present, and what can be added.

If the amperage printed on the main switch is 30 (found in many older houses with a two-wire system) or 60 (still common, and probably with a three-wire system) your house will need considerably more electrical service — which means adding new branch lines — before it can accommodate a normal complement of modern appliances. How much more service you need can be determined by subtracting your present power capacity from the capacity of recently built homes. Most new houses have a three-wire, 120/240-volt system. If the system has 60-amp service, it provides 14,400 watts of power. Better still, 100-amp service makes 24,000 available watts, which can handle a full range of modern appliances and lighting. The ideal, by present-day standards, is to have a three-wire, 120/240-volt system with 150-amp service. If the house is heated by electricity, it requires 200 amps. The terms "two-wire" and "three-wire" system indicate the number of individual wires wrapped in each cable. A two-wire cable has two wires, one covered with black insulation which is normally used as the hot line, and one covered with white insulation, which is always used as the grounding wire. When you run a two-wire cable and connect its black and white wires to a power source you will have one 120-volt circuit, and that is all you can ever have.

Three-wire cables contain the same white and black wires, plus a red wire that is also used as a hot line. The advantage of a three-wire system is that it offers the flexibility of creating three different circuits from a single cable. By connecting the two hot lines (black and red) you can have 240 volts of power, since each hot line can carry 120 volts. Alternatively, you can hook up the white wire with either the black or the red wire, and produce as many as two 120-volt circuits.

Relieving Overloaded Circuits

If your wiring list shows that you ought to have one or two new appliance circuits in the kitchen and a few more outlets throughout the house to meet your present needs, you can up-grade the system with minimum effort. In reality, there is no limit to the number of outlets that can be served by a branch circuit, but more than 10 will probably result in a lot of blown fuses. As a rule of thumb, if all the outlets in a room are already on the same circuit, it is best to put any new outlets on a new line. If you live in an older house, both your lighting and appliances are probably on the same circuits, which is now considered dangerous, so with an old electrical system, even minimal upgrading may include running both general purpose and major appliance lines.

Ideally, all the outlets and lights on each floor of a house should be evenly distributed between at least two 15-amp circuits, with each circuit serving no more than 400 to 600 square feet of floor space. If you are adding new circuits, keep the wall outlets on a circuit separate from lights, and space them between 7' and 12' apart.

Along with the 15-amp general purpose circuits, there should be at least two 20-amp special appliance circuits in the kitchen for handling the smaller appliances. You will rarely use more than two appliances simultaneously, so a pair of 20-amp lines should be adequate. You should also have separate 20-amp circuits for each major appliance and workshop power tool, and a separate 240-volt circuit for an electric range, an air conditioner drawing more than 1500 watts, the hot water heater and any other large power user.

Anytime you plan to do any major upgrading of a house electrical system, first ask your local power company if it can supply more service to the house. The utility company wants to sell more electricity, but it may not be equipped to do so. If the power company can accommodate you with more electricity, your next step is to ask the local building administration for any codes and regulations covering materials, and to get a permit to do the wiring. Many communities allow the homeowner to install new circuits only as far as the distribution box; the panel itself, which contains the fuses or circuit breakers, must be wired by a licensed electrician. Other locales insist that all work be inspected by an authorized expert.

Testing Circuits

The only way you can tell if an electrical circuit is working is to test it. There are several tools and methods that you can use for checking the electrical work in your house.

HOMEMADE HOT-LINE TESTER. Connect a 12" length of lamp cord to a light socket and tape the free end of each wire around a 4d (1½") finishing nail. Cut two 8" lengths of ½" dowel and wrap each nail to the ends of the dowels with electrician's tape. You want to leave ½" of the nails protruding beyond the ends of the dowels. Stick two or three strips of electrician's tape around the top of a 15-watt bulb (to keep it from shattering during use) and screw the bulb into the socket. As long as you always hold the probes of the tester by the wooden dowels, the unit is quite safe to use around live 120-volt circuits — but don't ever touch the bare nails while you are doing any testing.

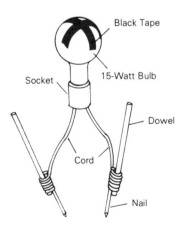

Black Tape

Socket

15-Watt Bulb

Dowel

Cord

Nail

Note the strips of electrician's tape, which will prevent the glass from shattering.

HOT-LINE NEON TESTER. You can buy a ready-made hot-line tester at any electrical supply or hardware store for about $1. The manufactured version of a hot-line tester has a tiny neon light that can handle between 60 and 500 volts without burning out.

TESTING A HOT LINE. You can use either hot-line tester to find out whether an outlet is "live" by simply pushing its probes into each slot of the receptacle. If the outlet is live, the light will go on.

TESTING A GROUND. Every outlet in the home must be properly grounded. The white grounding wire that is part of the electrical cable feeding the receptacle box is supposed to be connected to the longer of the two slots in the outlet (usually the left-hand slot). But you'll be surprised at how often receptacles are improperly wired.

Insert one probe of the tester into the long (grounded) slot and touch the other probe to the cover plate or center mounting screw of the outlet. (If these are painted, remove the plate and touch the probe to the side of the box.) If the box is properly grounded, the bulb will *not* go on — sticking the probe in the grounded side of the box does not complete a circuit, but merely extends the ground wire.

Conversely, if the probe is shifted to the shorter (right) slot in the outlet and the other probe is touched to a metal part of the box, the light should go on. If the bulb does not light, the grounding wire is either broken or improperly connected.

TESTING A WHOLE CIRCUIT. To test an entire house circuit, open the distribution box and remove the metal plate that covers the fuses or circuit breakers. With two-wire service, the white wire of the main cable coming into the house is connected to the white wires from each branch circuit, usually along a ground bus bar. Each white wire is attached to the bar with terminal screws at the bottom or side of the box. The black lead from each circuit cable is connected to the fuse socket or breaker. If you have a three-wire service, there are either two black leads, or one black and one red, in addition to the white wire. There are 120 volts between the white wires and any one of the hot lines. But between any two blacks or between a black and a red wire, there are either 208 or 240 volts.

If you are using a homemade tester on a 120/240, three-wire system, you can touch the probes to any combination of wires as long as one of them is white. But if you put the probes on any two hot lines in a three-wire service, the tester light will blow out in a few seconds because it will get too much voltage. The neon tester can be used on any voltage between 60 and 500 volts, and will not be harmed by touching a pair of hot lines in a three-wire system. Actually, higher voltage will only make the neon light glow more brightly. Follow this testing procedure:

1) Touch one probe of the tester to a white line.

2) Touch the other probe to one side of the fuse (or breaker) socket, then the other. If electricity is flowing through the socket, the light will go on each time. If the fuse is blown or the breaker is faulty, the light will go on when the hot side of the fuse socket is touched, but not when you touch the threaded part of the socket.

ELECTRICAL EQUIPMENT

All the electrical equipment such as tape, connectors, cables, fuses, terminals, wire nuts, cords and wires used in home electrical work must meet a prescribed standard of safety and durability. The standard, as recognized by the electrical industry, is established by the Underwriters Laboratories, Inc. (UL).

The UL is a nonprofit organization that tests electrical equipment in accordance with strict rules and regulations. The testing is rigorous, and any appliance or piece of equipment that carries a UL label comes with the assurance that it has been proven to be safe when used under its rated operating conditions.

Cables

Both armored and nonmetallic sheathed cables are used extensively in homes all over the United States. Both are flexible, easy to work with and can be purchased with two, three or four color-coded wires that come in almost any length; standard rolls are 25', 50', 100' and 250'. All two-wire cables have one black wire and one white. The wire covered with black insulation is always used as the hot wire, while the white one is the ground. Three-wire cables have a third, red-covered, wire, which is also hot.

The white wires are intended to provide a continuous ground from outlet to outlet all through the house until they reach the grounding bus bar in the distribution box which is connected to a water pipe. The nonmetallic sheathed cable and the newest armored cables have an additional bare wire used for grounding. Wherever possible, the bare wire should be attached directly to the receptacle box.

Before you buy any kind of cable for your house, check your local electrical code for any restrictions on its use.

ARMORED (BX) CABLE.   Armored cable may have two, three or four wires, plus the bare "drain" (for grounding) wire. Each of the electrical wires is separately insulated and wrapped in paper before it is encased in a spiral galvanized steel sheathing. Armored cable, commonly known as **BX**, is a lot harder to work with than nonmetallic sheathed cable, but in some locales it is the only cable you are allowed to use. You have to cut the metal sheathing with a hacksaw, and the cable is difficult to pull through a wall because the sheathing tends to catch on the framing and is not very flexible. Armored cable should not be used in damp or underground places, where it will eventually rust and corrode.

To prepare BX cable, follow this procedure:

1) Before connecting the cable to an outlet or switch, strip the end of its metal armor. Approximately 8″ to 12″ from the end of the cable, make a diagonal cut in the armor with a fine-toothed hacksaw blade. Rotate the cable as the cut is being made until the armor is completely cut. Do the cutting by hand and be very careful not to slice into the insulated wires inside. Once the armor is severed, twist it until it breaks and can be pulled off the wires.

2) Unwind the paper around each wire until you are past the end of the remaining armor, and tear off the paper. Then bend the bare aluminum grounding wire back and wrap it around the outside of the cable armor. If there are any bent edges where you cut the armor, straighten them with pliers.

Insert a red fiber bushing around the wires and jam it inside the end of the armor. The bushing is a required protection against the edges of the armor cutting into any insulation around the wires, and is readily available at any store that carries electrical supplies. Its head will be visible at the end of the cable and can be seen through a slot in the receptacle box; if an inspector does not find a bushing on every cable he will not approve the job.

3) With the bushing in place, insert the wires through a BX cable connector and tighten the retaining screw against the metal armor to lock the connector in position.

Now measure how much wire you need to reach the terminals on the outlet or switch going in the box, and allow a generous loop of wire that can be bent around the inside of the box beside or behind the switch or receptacle. It is easier to handle a little extra wire than to have to rerun a whole cable just because the wire was cut too short. Remove ½″ to 1″ of insulation from the end of each wire. Use a knife to slice the insulation at an angle as if sharpening a pencil, so that you don't nick the copper wire inside.

4) Insert the threaded end of the connector through a knock-out hole in the receptacle box and tighten the connector locknut against the side of the box to hold the cable firmly. The cable is now ready to be connected to terminals on the receptacle or switch.

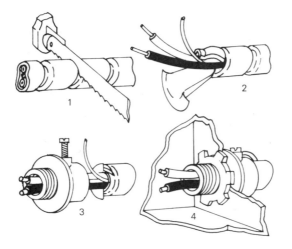

The four steps in preparing BX cable.

NONMETALLIC (NM) SHEATHED CABLE.   This is the least expensive and easiest cable to work with. It has either a fibrous or plastic sheath. If it is marked **NMC**, it may be used in dry, damp and wet locations, because all its wires are individually insulated and embedded in plastic. All new nonmetallic sheathed cables contain a bare ground wire, although in older house installations you may find **NM** cable without it.

To prepare any NM cable, follow this procedure:

1) NM cable is easily stripped because its sheath can be cut with wire cutters or a knife. Slit the sheath, keeping your knife point between the wires so that you don't damage any of the insulation on the wires.

2) After you have slit about 6″ or 8″ of the cable, fold the two halves of the sheath back and cut them off.

3) Remove the paper and filler from around the wires. The bare grounding wire should not be cut off.

4) Strip about 1″ of insulation from the ends of the copper wires, and insert the cable through an NM connector. Tighten the clamping screws.

5) Put the connector through a knockout hole in the receptacle box and tighten the locknut on the threaded end of the connector.

The five steps in preparing nonmetallic cable.

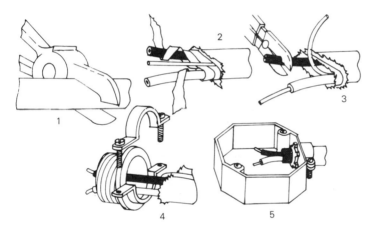

GROUNDING THE RECEPTACLE BOX. The bare wire found in every NM cable and all new BX cable is used for grounding the receptacle box. You can ground a box in any one of four ways, although the method you use may be dictated by your local electrical code.

1) Wrap several turns of the bare wire around the tip of the nonmetallic sheath so that it can fit under the cable clamp in the box. Then, when you tighten the connector over the wrapped

wire, the grounding connection is completed. If you wrap the bare wire around the armor of a **BX** cable, the cable and box are automatically grounded as soon as the cable clamp is tightened on the armor.

2) The bare wire can be attached directly to the receptacle box by wrapping it around a grounding setscrew placed in one of the tapped holes in the back of the box.

3) If there are several cables entering a box, all their grounding wires can be twisted and held together by a pressure-type lug which is then attached to the back of the box with a screw. Even old switch and receptacle boxes have tapped holes in their backs so that grounding wires can be attached to them with machine screws.

4) Run the wire through a slot in the top or side of the special grounding clip, then force the clip over the edge of the box by tapping it lightly with pliers or the handle of a screwdriver. *Caution:* If the grounding wire is inside the box it should be taped, or at least bent, well away from the electrical wires so it cannot touch any of the outlet or switch terminals.

The four typical ways of connecting the bare grounding wire in cable.

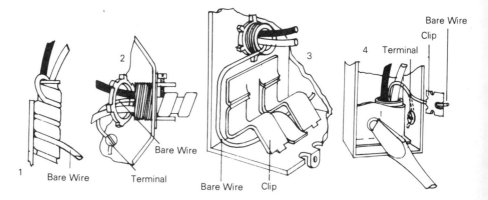

Wires

The amount of electricity that can flow through a wire depends on the wire's diameter. Wire diameter is established by a system known as the Brown & Sharpe Gauge, also called the American Wire Gauge (AWG). Wire gauges range from #40, which is only 3.1 mils in diameter, all the way up to #4/0, which is nearly ½" in diameter. The higher the wire number, the thinner the wire and the less current it is able to carry. Number 14, #12 and #10 wires are used for most house circuits, while #16 and #18 are customarily used for doorbells and intercoms. The smaller-gauge wires are always twisted together in strands for flexibility, so they can be used as fixture wires, lamp cords and small appliance connections.

Receptacle (Outlet) Boxes

Every house circuit has one or more receptacle (outlet) boxes. All boxes are the same, but may contain outlets or switches or both, or be used as a junction where wires are connected. The receptacle box is a small metal cabinet that may be rectangular, square, octagonal or round, and has a number of knockout holes stamped in its sides. You can remove the knockouts by tapping them with a screwdriver and hammer. Boxes intended for house

Knockouts

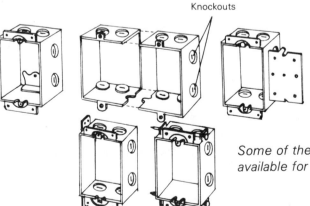

Some of the receptable boxes available for electrical work.

wiring have two knockout sizes. One size is large enough for a **BX** or **NM** connector. The smaller size allows the cable to enter the box only through built-in clamps.

The boxes are a marvel of design. They have more knockouts in every side than are ever necessary. Some of them have detachable sides, so two or more boxes can be joined to form a larger assembly that might, for example, house a row of switches. Spanners can be used to hold the boxes firmly between ceiling joists. Name your problem and there is a box, or some way of converting a box, to solve it.

Cable Connectors

BX CONNECTORS. The connectors used to attach **BX** cable are small tubes, each of which has a setscrew at one end, and is threaded at the other to receive a flanged locknut. Follow this procedure to install a **BX** connector:

1) Push the base of the connector over the exposed end of the cable and press it tightly against the front edge of the bushing inserted around the wires.

2) Tighten the setscrew against the armor to hold the connector on the cable.

3) Push the wires and threaded end of the connector through a knockout in the receptable box, and screw the locknut to it inside the box. When the nut is as tight as you can get it, hold the blade of a screwdriver against one of the notches in its rim and tap it clockwise with a hammer until it is absolutely tight.

NM CONNECTORS. The connectors used with **NM** cable are threaded tubes that fit over the exposed end of the cable and are held in place by flat clamps in back. To install these connectors, follow this procedure:

1) Squeeze the clamp against the cable with a pair of set-screws.

2) Put the threaded end of the connector through a knockout in the box.

3) Screw a flanged locknut to the connector against the inside of the box, and tap the nut tight with a screwdriver blade and hammer.

ANGLE CONNECTORS. You can use these with either **BX** or **NM** cable when the cable approaches a box at a right angle. The elbow protrudes about ½″ from the side of the box, clamps the cable and helps ease the wires into the box.

Cable Support

All cable must be firmly attached to a solid structural support at least every 5′ and within 1′ of every box it enters. You can buy U-shaped metal straps that are nailed around the cable and into a stud or wall, or use staples. Staples must be positioned with care if you are working with **NM** cable so that they do not penetrate the wire or damage its sheath.

Switches

A switch is designed to open or close the circuit to which it is attached, so it is fundamentally a mechanical device operated by a button, lever or dial. The switch is inserted into a circuit in such a way that it will interrupt the flow of electricity by causing a break in the hot line. There are several kinds of switches, each accomplishing the same task in a different way.

SINGLE-POLE TOGGLE SWITCH. This is the most widely used wall switch. It is designed to fit in a receptable box and has two terminal screws. The words "off" and "on" are printed on opposite sides of its handle. To install a single-pole toggle switch, cut the hot wire in the circuit cable and connect each open end of the wire to one of the two terminal screws on the switch. When the switch is closed, or on, current will flow through the unit. When it is open, or off, the circuit is broken and no electricity can enter the unit.

DOUBLE-POLE SWITCH.   It is often desirable, when you are controlling heavy-duty appliances, to open both wires leading to the unit. The double-pole switch has four terminals, two for the black (and/or red) wires as well as two for the white wires, plus the words "off" and "on" on its handles. It is installed by connecting both the hot and ground wires in the circuit to the proper terminal screws on the switch.

Left: How to hook up a double switch.
Right: How to connect a single switch.

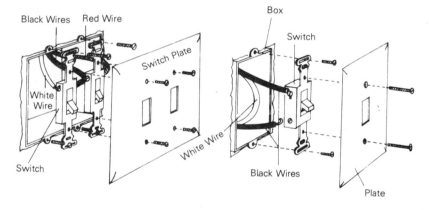

THREE-WAY SWITCHES.   It is sometimes more convenient if you can turn a light on or off from two different places, such as in both the garage and the house, or at both ends of a stairway. For this operation you need a three-way switch, technically known as the single-pole double-throw switch. The "three-way" part of its name comes from the fact that it has three terminals, and the words "off" and "on" do *not* appear on its lever. When you wire a pair of three-way switches to a light, the black wire from the source is connected to the common terminal on one of the switches. The terminal is usually marked "C" or is painted a dark color. First run a black line from the marked terminal on the other switch to the light. Then connect two wires, called travellers, to the remaining (light colored) terminals on the switches. The grounding white wire goes from the light directly back to the source of power to complete the circuit.

If the switches are properly wired and both switch handles are up or down, the light will be on; it can be turned off only when one of the switch handles is moved to the position opposite that of the other handle.

SOME OTHER SWITCHES. You can find all kinds of switches. Some can be turned on or off only with a key. Others have their handles held in one position by a spring, so as soon as you release the lever it returns to that position. Silent mercury switches can be installed anywhere a switch click is objectionable. Dimmers are available for either incandescent or fluorescent lamps.

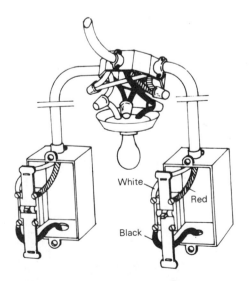

White

Red

Black

The connections for a pair of two-way switches controlling the same lamp.

CONNECTIONS

All splices and joints in every house circuit must be made in an electrical box which may contain a junction, receptacle or switch. But once the cables enter a box there are several ways of putting the wires together.

Wire Nut Connection

The invention of the wire nut has eliminated soldering in house wiring. The wire nut is a hollow, cone-shaped, insulated connector with a coil of spring wire inside it. Wire nuts come in all sizes and you can buy them to fit whatever gauge and number of wires you are putting together. First twist the wires together with pliers, then screw the cap down over the bare ends until it overlaps the insulation of the wires. The internal spring grips the joint and holds the wires tightly together. Wire nuts are easily removed by unscrewing, but they should not slip off when you pull at them. Small wire nuts can also be used with stranded wire.

Twist and Tape Connection

The simplest method of joining two copper wires is to strip about an inch of insulation from the ends of the wires, twist them together, then wrap the bare wires with plastic tape, extending it over the insulation of each wire.

Spliced Joint

If two wires are to be spliced, cut them to different lengths. The wires of a lamp cord, for example, should be cut to lengths that vary by several inches, and the ends stripped. The ends are then twisted together and each splice is taped individually; finally, both splices are wrapped with a second layer of tape.

Screw Terminal Connections

To connect to a unit that has screw terminals, strip about an inch of wire and bend it into a hook with long-nosed pliers. Now hook the loop over the screw in a clockwise position so that when the screw is tightened, the wire will be forced in the same direction as the turn of the screw. Pinch the wire loop closed with pliers before the screw is tightened.

The wires in many appliances are attached via a small lug at the end of the wire. The lug is a U-shaped, flat piece of metal with a hollow barrel which slides over the end of a wire and is then squeezed tightly with either pliers or a crimping tool. The lug prongs fit on either side of a terminal screw, and by tightening the screw you can complete the connection.

The four basic wire connections used in home electrical work.

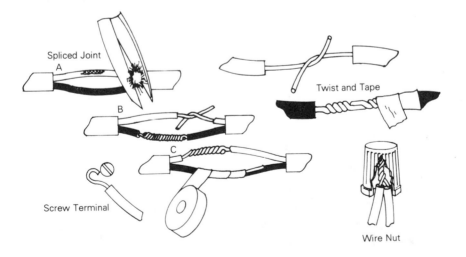

Spliced Joint
A

Twist and Tape

B

C

Screw Terminal

Wire Nut

INSTALLING A NEW BRANCH CIRCUIT

A branch circuit consists of a two-, three- or four-wire cable that begins at the house distribution box and serves one or more outlets and/or switches and light fixtures. The procedure for installing a branch circuit is not difficult, but you may be in for some frustrating problems trying to pull the cable through your walls.

Installing a First-Floor Circuit

If you can work from the basement, find where the cable will emerge from the wall, and drill a hole up through the floor into the soleplate of the wall. Your drill will need an 18" extension bit, and you will have to angle it into the underside of the floor so that it comes out inside the wall. In order to find exactly where to drill, you will have to do some measuring in both the basement and the floor above. Once the hole is drilled, position an opening for the new outlet in the first-floor wall and cut it ⅛" larger than the dimensions of the receptacle box. It should be at the same level as the other boxes in the room (12" to 18" from the floor).

If the wall is lath and plaster, chip away the plaster in the center of the box outline until you uncover one complete lath. Center the electrical box over the lath, mark the outline of the box on the wall and chisel away the plaster inside the outline. Do not damage the lath. When the whole lath is exposed inside the outline of the box, cut away all of the exposed wood with a coping saw. The center lath will be completely removed, but only half the width of the top and bottom laths will be cut. Be careful not to break the top and bottom laths, because you need that wood to hold the screws that anchor the box to the wall.

If the wall is wallboard, mark the box outline anywhere between studs and cut out the wallboard with a utility or saber saw, making sure the hole is no more than ⅛" larger than the box. There are two accessory arrangements for holding an electrical box in the wall opening. One is a mounting clamp that squeezes the edge of the drywall when it is tightened with a setscrew. The other is a thin metal support bar that fits on either side of the box and has tabs that can be bent over the front edge of the box.

The sturdiest way of installing the box is to attach it to a stud. You can buy a box with metal flanges so that it can be nailed or screwed to the side or front of the stud (provided enough of the wall is removed so you have space to work in).

How to cut and fit a receptacle box in a plaster and lath wall.

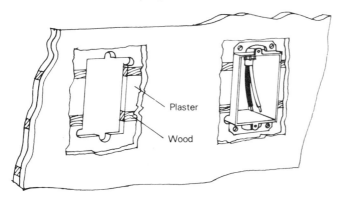

Plaster

Wood

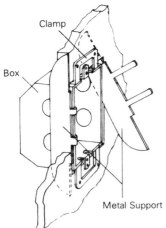

Clamp

Box

Metal Support Plates

Receptacle boxes can be mounted between studs in a drywall using either clamps or metal supports that are fitted in the hole and bent over the sides of the box.

Running Cable

Once the hole for the receptacle is cut, you can insert the cable into the wall. If your wiring is being done in new construction and the walls are still open, you can run wires anyplace without any particular difficulty. But if the wall is already completed, channels must be chipped in the plaster or drywall so you can bring your cables around the studs and spacers. You can replaster the channels once the cables are in place.

When they run from one floor to the next, the cables must pass through the soleplates, flooring and top plates of each wall. The simplest procedure is to remove the baseboard and drill diagonally down through the baseplate, the floor and the top plate in the wall below, using an 18″ bit extension. With luck, you can feed your cable down through the hole all the way to the floor of the room below. However, the cable will most likely run into spacers between the studs, at which point you will have to chisel a channel out of the wall.

Connecting Receptacles

When your cable is run and its ends protrude from each of the receptable holes, strip the cable and clamp it in the receptacle boxes. When all the cables entering the box have been connected and their bare grounding wires are properly connected (see page 156), push the box into its recess. Screw the box mounting screws into the lath if the wall is a plaster and lath wall. If the wall is a drywall construction, use sheet metal strips or mounting clamps to secure the unit in place.

Installing the Receptacle or Switch

Follow this procedure:

1) Strip 1″ of insulation from the end of each of the cable wires.

2) When connecting a receptacle, attach the black wire to the brass-coated terminal screw on the side of the receptacle, and the white wire to the silver nickel-plated screw. When connecting a switch, cut *only* the black wire and attach each end to a terminal screw.

3) Connect a short length of either bare or insulated wire from the green terminal on the receptacle to the box to insure a proper secondary ground.

4) Bend all the wires inside the box until the mounting tabs on the top and bottom of the receptacle or switch are flush against the front of the box.

5) Attach the receptacle to the box with the two #6-32 flat-head screws that come with the receptacle.

6) Install the faceplate. If the plate appears crooked, remove it and loosen the screws holding the receptacle to the box. Realign the receptacle and tighten the screws again, then replace the plate.

Top: How to install a single receptacle.
Bottom: How to install a double receptacle;
note where the wires are connected.

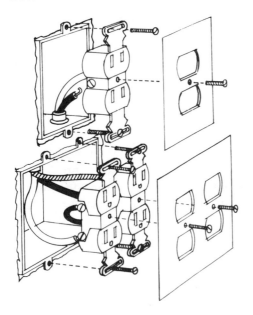

Replacing Switches or Receptacles

If a switch or receptacle doesn't work or causes a fuse or circuit breaker to blow, it must be replaced. Switches and receptacles are so inexpensive they are not worth attempting to repair.

REPLACING A SINGLE UNIT.   Follow this procedure:

1) Remove the circuit's fuse or turn off the circuit breaker.
2) Unscrew the faceplate.
3) Pull the switch or receptacle out of the box and loosen the terminal screws to disengage the wires.
4) Attach the wires to their proper terminals on the new unit (black wire to brass screw and white wire to silver screw for an outlet; black wire to each of the terminals on a switch).
5) When replacing an old receptacle with a new three-wire grounded type, join a short length of wire from the green ground terminal on the receptacle directly to the side of the box with a clip, or into the back of the box with a machine screw.
6) Push the receptacle or switch back into the box and screw it in place. Put on the faceplate.
7) Turn on the fuse or circuit breaker.

REPLACING A MULTIPLE UNIT.   The procedure for replacing a multiple or combination switch or outlet is the same as for a single unit. However, you will find terminal screws on each side of the unit that allow the halves of the unit to be fed either separately or with the same circuit wires. If you have more than one circuit entering the box, you can give each unit its own power source. If you want all the units to feed off a single power source, their terminals must be connected by jumper wires, unless the unit has metal links, which can be twisted off with pliers for separate feeds. When replacing a switch or receptacle, note how the old unit is connected; you will find it helpful to make a sketch of the terminals and wire colors.

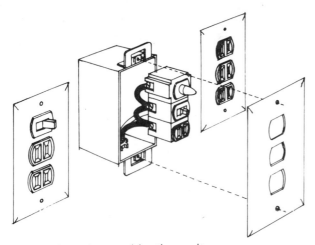

Installation of a combination unit.

OVERHEAD FIXTURES

Putting in an overhead fixture, aside from the fatigue of having to reach up all the time, is no more difficult than installing a receptacle. The boxes used in ceilings are square, octagonal or round, and can be purchased with flanges that hold the box between joists. There are also a variety of both solid and adjustable hangers that can either be nailed between ceiling beams or allowed to rest directly on the ceiling lath. Select a box that meets the conditions and needs of the job you are doing, and connect the cable to it before positioning the box in its hole. If there is already a box in the ceiling, it may not be equipped to accept the mounting assembly that comes with the fixture. The screws, bolts and pipes used to hang ceiling fixtures vary according to the unit and its manufacturer, but they can usually be exchanged for a different system.

Follow this installation procedure:

1) If there is an existing outlet, shut off the electricity. Otherwise, mark the place in the ceiling where the box will be situated.

2) Cut a hole in the ceiling, then use a chisel or a utility saw to trim away any wood or other backing to the plaster or drywall that is visible inside the penciled outline of the box.

3) Fish cable from either a junction or receptacle box, or directly from the distribution box, to the hole.

4) Connect the black wire or wires of the fixture with the black cable wire, using wire nuts to join the wires (see page 168). Attach the white wire in the fixture to the white cable wire in the same manner.

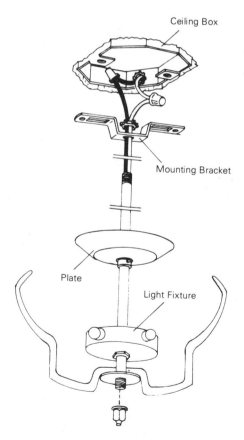

Ceiling Box

Mounting Bracket

Plate

Light Fixture

Anatomy of a ceiling fixture. The parts used for hanging will vary according to type of fixture.

5) Hang the fixture from the box. Make certain you don't pinch any of the wires with any metal in the fixture or box — you don't want to break or damage them. If there is any possibility of damage, protect the wires before you hang the fixture by wrapping them in electrician's tape.

DOOR SIGNALING SYSTEM

Doorbells and buzzers operate on so low a voltage that people used to run them on 1½-volt batteries. But it is more convenient to install a small step-down transformer rated at six to 10 volts (and five watts). The transformer is connected to one of your 120-volt circuits, but it reduces the voltage to the point at which it is quite safe to work on a door signaling system without shutting off the source of power.

Modern transformers have a threaded flange device on one side so you can clamp them into the knockout opening of either the fuse cabinet or a receptacle box. There are two primary wire leads at the back of the unit which you connect to the house

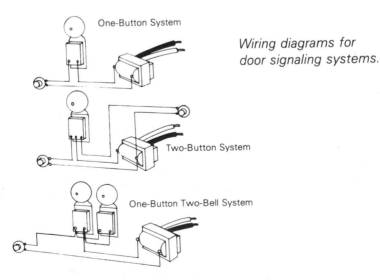

Wiring diagrams for door signaling systems.

circuit. The front (or secondary side) of the unit has a pair of screw terminals for connecting the bell circuit wiring.

The wire size used with signaling systems is normally #18, although this may vary from #16 to #22, depending on the electrical load and the length of the run.

Types of Systems

PUSH BUTTONS. Probably 99% of the problems that occur with any house signaling system are in the push buttons. The internal parts of the button are often made of iron, and these eventually rust or corrode. You can clean the metal contacts with fine sandpaper, but you'll find it is easier to buy a new button and install it.

BELLS, BUZZERS AND CHIMES. You can find dozens of different bells, buzzers and chimes on the market, but they all operate in about the same manner. Bells and buzzers consist of a coil of wire which, when electricity flows through it, energizes an electromagnetic rod that strikes the buzzer or bell. Whatever unit you buy, it is designed to last for years and when it finally does stop working, it is easier to replace than to repair.

Installing Systems

If you are replacing an old system, use the existing wires to pull the new wires through the house. Either separate wires or a two-wire cable may be used as long as all of your connections are made carefully.

PUSH BUTTON. If there are no old wires to pull the new wires through to the outside of the door frame, drill through the door frame at an angle that slants away from the door. The hole should be between ¼″ and ¾″ in diameter, depending on the size of the button being installed. There is a hollow space, or *bay,* between the door casing and the double studs that make up the interior frame of the door. A second hole must be drilled into the bottom of the door frame through the cellar ceiling, and the button wires fished through the two holes.

Connect the wires to the two terminals on the back of the button and screw the button to the door frame. One of the wires goes directly to the transformer. The other leads to the bell or buzzer. A third wire returns from the bell or buzzer back to the transformer. As you run the wires between the button and the signal and into the basement, tack them to joists (or wherever you can) with insulated staples.

The transformer should be connected through a knockout in a receptacle box so you can connect its primary wires to the house circuit wires (white to white, black to black) inside the box. You can hang the junction box from a joist or wall, but it should be as close as you can get it to the fuse box or distribution panel. Better yet, insert the transformer through a knockout in the side of a fuse box, shut off the main house switch and wire the transformer directly to a fuse socket. When the junction box and transformer are in place, connect the wires from the bell or buzzer and button to the secondary terminals on the front of the transformer.

INSTALLING CHIMES. The procedure for installing a set of door chimes is the same as for doorbells or buzzers. However, the transformer for chimes must provide 14 to 18 volts and 10 watts.

In order to install the chimes themselves, first remove the face cover. Pull the wires through the hole in the back of the unit, and hang the unit on the wall. Then connect the wires to their correct terminals, which usually are clearly marked by the manufacturer.

LIGHTING REPAIRS

Incandescent Bulbs

Bulbs come in hundreds of sizes, colors and shapes, but they all consist of a wire filament inside a glass bulb that is filled with an inert gas — usually a mixture of nitrogen and argon. There is no way to repair an incandescent bulb.

What you can repair are the lamps that hold incandescent bulbs. If a wall or ceiling fixture fails to work, you can take it apart and examine its connections. If the bulb in a lamp flickers or does not go on, first be sure the bulb is properly screwed into its base and that the plug is firmly in its outlet. The best way to check a bulb is to screw it into a socket that you know is in working order. Next check the branch circuit fuse or circuit breaker to be sure that power is reaching the lamp, and also make sure the cord plug is not broken. If you are sure all these elements are in working order, unplug the lamp and dismantle it.

REPAIRING LAMPS. Lamps look different, but they are all put together in the same way — with a socket and various bottles, balls, pieces of metal or bric-a-brac strung on a length of pipe that is ⅜″ in diameter. To repair a lamp, follow this procedure:

1) Pry off the protective felt cover on the base of the lamp, using a screwdriver or knife.

2) With a wrench or pliers, loosen the nut attached to the bottom of the long metal tube that extends the length of the unit. You may find there is some sort of weight attached to the base which must also be removed from the base.

3) Withdraw the tube from the top of the lamp base and unscrew the socket from the top of the tube by rotating it counter-clockwise.

4) Press the bottom of the socket and pull or twist it off the socket base. Slide the paper insulating sleeve off the socket. The socket will lift off the bottom of the unit.

5) Loosen the terminals on either side of the socket and remove the wires. If the socket is being replaced, connect one wire to each of the terminals on the new socket. If you are also replacing the cord, pull the old cord out of the tube and run the new one into it, then connect the wires to the socket and reassemble the lamp.

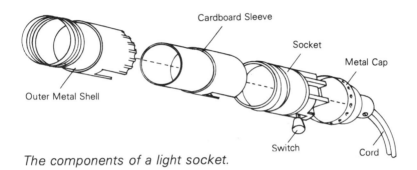

The components of a light socket.

REPAIRING CORDS AND PLUGS. The cords used on both appliances and lamps get a lot of wear. Their insulation often cracks or wears through to the bare wire, and even breaks. They should be inspected frequently and repaired or replaced at the first sign of deterioration. All cords consist of two wires embedded in rubber or plastic insulation, which is then given a rubber, cloth or plastic covering.

Whenever you replace a cord, be certain the wire gauge is the same as, or larger than, the wire in the cord being replaced. Remove the insulation from the ends of both wires and connect one wire to each of the appliance terminals. When attaching the plug, insert both wires through the base of the plug and, if possible, tie them in an underwriter's knot before connecting them to the plug terminal screws. The knot will prevent the wires from being pulled off their terminal screws when the cord is yanked out of a receptacle. When you place a bare wire around a terminal screw, first twist the strands together, then wrap them clockwise around the screw, and be sure that no frayed strands touch the wire around the opposite terminal after the screws are tightened.

How to tie the underwriter's knot.

Fluorescent Lights

The basic fluorescent light is comprised of a glass tube up to $1\frac{1}{2}''$ in diameter and as much as 8' long, although some types are circular or U-shaped. Fluorescent lamps consist of either a circular or rectangular metal housing containing the lamp holders, ballast and starter. Actually there are two types of fixtures usually found in the home. The older type requires a starter to turn on the lamp. The latest fixtures are called *rapid-start* or *trigger-start,* and are connected directly to the house circuit. When turned on, the rapid-start lamps come on gradually over several seconds and do not flicker or flash as do the older, starter-type lamps.

LAMP HOLDERS. The lamp holders, or sockets, on a straight tube fixture extend at right angles from each end of the metal housing to receive the double pins on each end of the tube. Place the pins in the slots of the socket and rotate the tube about 90° until it fits snugly in place. The pins on a circular tube are plugged into a socket, and the tube is held in place by spring clips.

STARTER. One of the sockets in a straight tube unit has a recess (just below the lamp) that accepts the starter, which is a small metal canister about 1¼″ long, with two small disks protruding from one end. To install a starter, push it into its socket and give it a clockwise twist until it locks in place. The starter socket is wired directly to the ballast. The socket for the starter on a circular lamp is in the face of the lamp housing, within the ring of the circular tube. Starters burn out and must be replaced.

BALLAST. This is essentially a transformer, which increases the line voltage to help light the tube, then limits the flow of current so that the tube will not burn out.

Starter-type (above) and rapid-start (below) fluorescent lights.

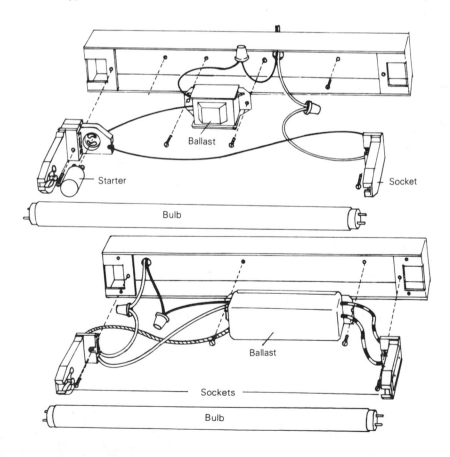

TEN

Beyond the Basic Tools

DURING THE COURSE OF COMPLETING VARIOUS RE-pairs you will probably acquire such useful tools as a utility knife, a combination plier-wrench, a utility saw, perhaps a nail punch and an electrician's multipurpose tool, which can strip insulation, cut wire, crimp connectors and measure wire diameters. Each of these tools will be a welcome addition to your basic repair kit and each is worthy of the money you spend for it. But if you become hooked on making repairs around your home, you may find yourself moving toward the many pleasures of assembling various materials into useful, or just plain decorative, objects.

Build a simple bookcase or two, and you may well begin to think about dadoed shelves, mitered frame corners and the craftsmanship of not a box with shelves, but a piece of furniture. To reach these heights of cabinetmaking, you must move into the realm of radial arm and table saws, drill presses, belt-disk sanders, routers, dado blades and molding heads. Each of these stationary power tools offers a guaranteed precision that automatically makes any tinkerer suddenly capable of turning out truly professional projects.

But working with stationary power tools requires money, time and space to work in. If you have those three elements at your disposal, there is no reason not to acquire whatever heavy equipment you fancy. A reasonable order of tool purchasing would begin with buying a *table saw* or a *radial arm saw,* both

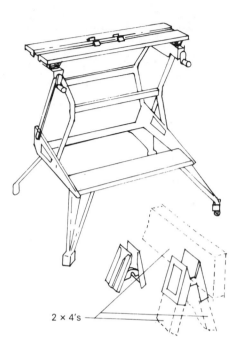

2 × 4's

A collapsible workbench-vise and sawhorse brackets.

of which cost about $300. Of the two, the radial arm offers the most versatility; but for absolute accuracy, the table saw is hard to match.

Following a power saw, $150 will buy you a good *belt-disk sander*. Sanding is a vital part of cabinetry; the standing sander is therefore an invaluable tool to have.

Next would come a *drill press* ($400), and from there on you can consider such tools as a *band saw* and *joiner-planers* ($300 each).

Purchasing stationary tools is a long step into cabinetmaking. There is a less expensive stage that will bring you almost as much satisfaction while enabling you to complete many projects.

The immediate extension of your basic tool kit should be a stable place to work. You can purchase two sets of *sawhorse brackets* ($5 per set) which are nailed to the ends of 2x4's to give you a pair of collapsible sawhorses. A more expensive but infinitely more versatile work table is one of the new, portable *workbench-vises,* which can be purchased for around $70.

With a place to work on, you can begin to concern yourself with the two most important elements of assembling wood: cutting and joining. The tools you need most are the circular power saw and the router, in that order.

Circular power saws are designated according to the diameters of their blades, which range from 6½″ to 8½″. Buy a 7¼″ saw, and also a set of 3½″ *dado blades.* Given the proper blade, the saw will cut anything, including masonry. It is designed to rip a straight line through any board in short order and, with a few hours of practice, you will not only be able to cut bevels, miters and rips, but gentle curves as well. Then you can put on the dado blades and suddenly you will be able to rout, dado, rabbet and cut out a host of highly professional cabinetmaking joints. The dado set is really several blades and cutters which you assemble on the saw arbor so that you can cut a dado or plough that is anywhere from ⅛″ to ¹³⁄₁₆″ wide, and as deep as you wish.

A circular power saw and 3½″ dado blade set.

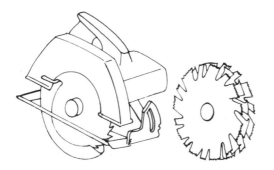

What the circular saw and dado blades can't do, the *router* can. A good machine will cost about $50, and the bits are as much as $10 each. Routers are high-speed cutters and take some learning to handle effectively, but with them you can make all kinds of fancy cuts and scrollwork, as well as rout out most known wood joints, including the classic dovetail. For that you need a $30 *dovetail template* — but then making drawers that will stay together forever becomes a natural part of all your woodworking.

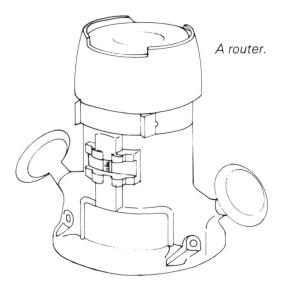

A router.

Given the kind of cutting and joining you are capable of with the hand power saw and router in your arsenal, you will also want to investigate the power sanders. The circular sanding disk that attaches to your drill is fine for the rough sanding and leveling of almost anything. If you want to cover a lot of territory quickly and evenly, spend the $60 for a *belt sander*. It is quick and powerful, and will sand off most of the circular marks made by your disk sander. If you are preparing wood for either paint or a clear finish, the *vibrating sander* ($20) is a good tool to have at your command.

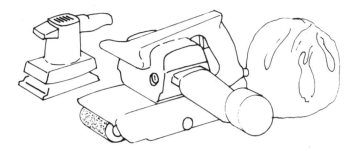

A vibrating sander (left) and belt sander (right).

The extension of electrical work is almost as endless, and certainly as refined, as cabinetmaking. To join the world of electronics and be able to build your own hi-fi equipment or computers from kits, repair your television set or get inside all the appliances in your home, you absolutely must have a *volt-ohms meter* (*multimeter*). You can spend anywhere from $15 to $150 for a meter, but $25 will get you a good, serviceable instrument. Once you are equipped to test your electrical work, you need only to expand your hand tools and learn how to use a *soldering gun*.

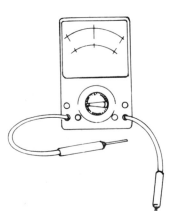

The volt-ohms meter, or multimeter.

As for plumbing, you can add a few more pipe wrenches and perhaps a *propane torch,* a *flaring tool, copper pipe cutter* and a *stock and die set.* With those few tools you can then go out and install the entire plumbing system in any house.

The options for broadening your interest in any of the manual arts are endless. But whether you buy them all or not, the best part of completing a repair or constructing a project is the quiet satisfaction of knowing you have done it — and if anything untoward should happen, you can do it again.

Index